ISSUES THAT CONCERN YOU

Eating Disorders

Julia Garbus, *Book Editor*

GREENHAVEN PRESS
A part of Gale, Cengage Learning

Farmington Hills, Mich • San Francisco • New York • Waterville, Maine
Meriden, Conn • Mason, Ohio • Chicago

Elizabeth Des Chenes, Director, Content Strategy
Douglas Dentino, Manager, New Product

© 2015 Greenhaven Press, a part of Gale, Cengage Learning

WCN: 01-100-101

Articles in Greenhaven Press anthologies are often edited for length to meet page requirements. In addition, original titles of these works are changed to clearly present the main thesis and to explicitly indicate the author's opinion. Every effort is made to ensure that Greenhaven Press accurately reflects the original intent of the authors. Every effort has been made to trace the owners of copyrighted material.

Cover image © yalayama/Shutterstock.com

LIBRARY OF CONGRESS CATALOGING-IN-PUBLICATION DATA

Eating disorders / Julia Garbus, book editor.
    pages cm. -- (Issues that concern you)
 Summary: "Issues That Concern You: Eating Disorders This series covers today's most current national and international issues and the most important opinions of the past and present. The purpose of the series is to introduce readers to all sides of contemporary controversies"-- Provided by publisher.
 Includes bibliographical references and index.
 ISBN 978-0-7377-7239-5 (hardback)
 1. Eating disorders. I. Garbus, Julia.
 RC552.E18E2821136 2015
 616.85'26--dc23
                                                                    2014021947

Printed in the United States of America
1 2 3 4 5 6 7 18 17 16 15 14

CONTENTS

Eating disorders are psychological illnesses that cause people to eat and think about food in abnormal ways that impair their health and everyday functioning. Eating disorders include anorexia (starving yourself), bulimia (binging and purging), binge eating disorder (frequently eating too much), and some much less common disorders such as pica (eating nonnutritious substances such as dirt) and rumination disorder (spitting food out). These diseases can be dangerous, causing physical problems throughout the body. And they can kill. It is estimated that more than 20 percent of people with untreated eating disorders die prematurely, either from health consequences of the illness or from suicide; this is the highest mortality rate of all mental illnesses. Anorexia is the most deadly disease affecting teen girls. For females between the ages of fifteen and twenty-four, the death rate from anorexia is twelve times higher than the death rate from all other causes of death combined.

Eating disorders have been documented as far back as the Middle Ages, when the wealthy would vomit during meals and then consume more. However, these diseases are becoming much more common. As many as 25 to 30 million Americans have suffered from an eating disorder. In every decade since 1930, the incidence of anorexia in teen girls ages fifteen to nineteen has increased. In the five-year period between 1988 and 1993, the rate of bulimia in women under forty tripled. Some of these rising numbers stem from greater awareness of these conditions and better diagnosis.

People of all ages are affected, but by far, teens are the hardest hit. Young adults account for 95 percent of all eating disorder sufferers. A 2011 *Archives of General Psychiatry* survey of more than ten thousand teens ages thirteen to eighteen sheds new light on how these diseases affect young people. The combined rate of anorexia and near-anorexia was about 1 percent, the bulimia rate was almost 1 percent, and the combined binge eating disorder and subthreshold binge eating disorder rate was about 4 percent. The median age that the disorders started was 12.5. Researchers found that eating disorders interfered with the teens' everyday lives, and suicidal thoughts or actions were common.

Some people think that eating disorders mostly affect a certain demographic—as writer Elizabeth Licorish puts it, "SWAGs," or skinny white affluent girls. It is true that white females have the highest rates of anorexia. However, experts say that other eating disorders are equally common among whites, Hispanics, African Americans, and Asians. In the *Archives of General Psychiatry* survey, Hispanic adolescents reported more bulimia than did the other groups, and ethnic minorities reported more instances of binge eating disorder than whites. How rich or poor the sufferers' families were made no difference. As for gender, 10 to 15 percent of eating disorder sufferers are male; there may be more, but fear of stigma discourages many boys and men from getting the help they need.

Health care professionals use a specific set of criteria to diagnose eating disorders and other mental disorders, contained in a volume called the *Diagnostic and Statistical Manual of Mental Disorders, Fifth Edition* (DSM-5). It is like a rule book, providing standardized definitions so that treatment professionals and others know they are using the same language. In DSM-5, published in May 2013, binge eating is listed as a separate disorder for the first time. Binge eating disorder is much more than eating too much every now and then. It involves binging at least once a week, as well as feeling very out of control and unhappy about one's eating. It is the most common eating disorder, and the outlook for sufferers is very good if they get help.

Anorexia is another common eating disorder, affecting almost 1 percent of women and 0.3 percent of men during their lives. It is characterized by self-starvation and excessive weight loss. Sufferers do not take in adequate food over a long period of time, leading to very low weight. They are extremely afraid of weight gain even though they are underweight; they perceive their body weight and shape differently than do nonsufferers, or they deny that their low weight is a problem. Anorexia is the hardest to treat of the eating disorders. One-third of sufferers will recover after first being treated, one-third will go back and forth between recovering and relapsing, and one-third will die.

Bulimia is more common than anorexia, affecting 1.5 percent of women and 0.5 percent of men. However, fewer sufferers are diagnosed, because people with bulimia are often normal weight, so others do not notice something is wrong. Bulimia has two components: binging (eating food excessively or compulsively, along with feeling out of control about it) and purging (getting rid of food). Purging can involve vomiting or other methods such as laxative use or excessive exercise. People with bulimia also focus too much on body shape and weight. Recovery rates are higher for those suffering from bulimia than anorexia. In the short term, 50 to 70 percent will recover, although up to half will relapse.

Eating disorders are not caused by one single factor, but instead by a combination of physical, emotional, social, and family issues. Genetics and environment also play a role. Researchers have discovered differences in brain function in people with certain disorders. Eating disorders often seem to go hand in hand with psychological issues such as low self-esteem, feelings of hopelessness and inadequacy, and perfectionism. People with eating disorders often have other serious mental issues; most of the eating-disordered teens in the 2011 DSM study also suffered from mood or anxiety disorders.

The authors quoted in this anthology discuss the roles of brain chemistry, genetics, environment, and culture on eating disorders. In addition, the volume explores different therapies and the most effective ways to treat eating disorders. The appendixes "What You Should Know About Eating Disorders" and "What You Should Do About Eating Disorders" provide additional information about the varying disorders and give suggestions for taking action. *Issues That Concern You: Eating Disorders* offers a resource for everyone interested in this topic.

ONE

Overview of Eating Disorders

National Institute of Mental Health

In the following viewpoint the National Institute of Mental Health (NIMH) provides an overview of the various types of eating disorders. The institute describes the characteristics of common eating disorders as well as effective treatment methods. Eating disorders are caused by a combination of genetic, biological, behavioral, psychological, and social factors, NIMH states. Researchers aim to better understand eating disorders by studying genetics, brain function, and risk factors that impact eating behavior. NIMH is part of the National Institutes of Health, a component of the US Department of Health and Human Services. NIMH focuses on transforming the understanding and treatment of mental illnesses in order to develop breakthroughs in prevention and recovery methods.

An eating disorder is an illness that causes serious disturbances to your everyday diet, such as eating extremely small amounts of food or severely overeating. A person with an eating disorder may have started out just eating smaller or larger amounts of food, but at some point, the urge to eat less or more spiraled out

National Institute of Metal Health, "Eating Disorders," NIH Publication No. 11-4901, US Department of Health and Human Services, 2011.

of control. Severe distress or concern about body weight or shape may also characterize an eating disorder.

Eating disorders frequently appear during the teen years or young adulthood but may also develop during childhood or later in life. Common eating disorders include anorexia nervosa, bulimia nervosa, and binge-eating disorder.

Eating disorders affect both men and women. . . .

Eating disorders are real, treatable medical illnesses. They frequently coexist with other illnesses such as depression, substance abuse, or anxiety disorders. Other symptoms, described in the next section, can become life-threatening if a person does not receive treatment. People with anorexia nervosa are 18 times more likely to die early compared with people of similar age in the general population.

What Are the Different Types of Eating Disorders?

Anorexia Nervosa

Anorexia nervosa is characterized by:

- Extreme thinness (emaciation)
- A relentless pursuit of thinness and unwillingness to maintain a normal or healthy weight
- Intense fear of gaining weight
- Distorted body image, a self-esteem that is heavily influenced by perceptions of body weight and shape, or a denial of the seriousness of low body weight
- Lack of menstruation among girls and women
- Extremely restricted eating.

Many people with anorexia nervosa see themselves as overweight, even when they are clearly underweight. Eating, food, and weight control become obsessions. People with anorexia nervosa typically weigh themselves repeatedly, portion food carefully, and eat very small quantities of only certain foods. Some people with anorexia nervosa may also engage in binge-eating followed by

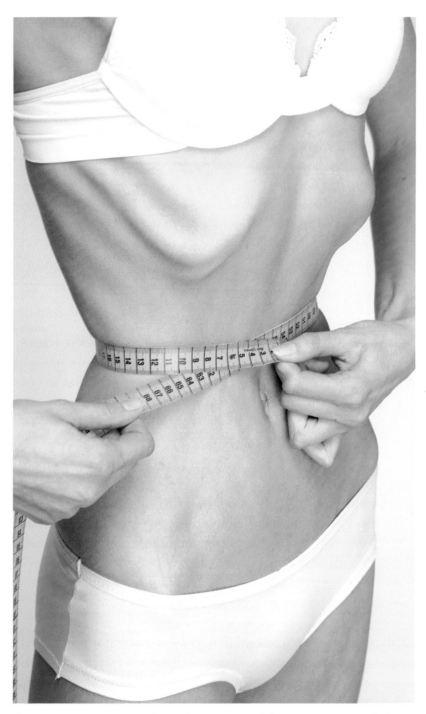

Anorexia nervosa is often characterized by emaciation of the body through lack of eating.

extreme dieting, excessive exercise, self-induced vomiting, and/ or misuse of laxatives, diuretics, or enemas.

Some who have anorexia nervosa recover with treatment after only one episode. Others get well but have relapses. Still others have a more chronic, or long-lasting, form of anorexia nervosa, in which their health declines as they battle the illness.

Other symptoms may develop over time, including:

- Thinning of the bones (osteopenia or osteoporosis)
- Brittle hair and nails
- Dry and yellowish skin
- Growth of fine hair all over the body (lanugo)
- Mild anemia and muscle wasting and weakness
- Severe constipation
- Low blood pressure, slowed breathing and pulse
- Damage to the structure and function of the heart
- Brain damage
- Multiorgan failure
- Drop in internal body temperature, causing a person to feel cold all the time
- Lethargy, sluggishness, or feeling tired all the time
- Infertility.

Bulimia Nervosa

Bulimia nervosa is characterized by recurrent and frequent episodes of eating unusually large amounts of food and feeling a lack of control over these episodes. This binge-eating is followed by behavior that compensates for the overeating such as forced vomiting, excessive use of laxatives or diuretics, fasting, excessive exercise, or a combination of these behaviors.

Unlike anorexia nervosa, people with bulimia nervosa usually maintain what is considered a healthy or normal weight, while some are slightly overweight. But like people with anorexia nervosa, they often fear gaining weight, want desperately to lose weight, and are intensely unhappy with their body size and shape. Usually, bulimic behavior is done secretly because it is often accompanied by feelings of disgust or shame. The binge-eating and purging cycle happens anywhere from several times a week to many times a day.

Other symptoms include:

- Chronically inflamed and sore throat
- Swollen salivary glands in the neck and jaw area
- Worn tooth enamel, increasingly sensitive and decaying teeth as a result of exposure to stomach acid
- Acid reflux disorder and other gastrointestinal problems
- Intestinal distress and irritation from laxative abuse
- Severe dehydration from purging of fluids
- Electrolyte imbalance (too low or too high levels of sodium, calcium, potassium, and other minerals), which can lead to heart attack.

Binge-eating disorder

With binge-eating disorder a person loses control over his or her eating. Unlike bulimia nervosa, periods of binge-eating are not followed by purging, excessive exercise, or fasting. As a result, people with binge-eating disorder often are overweight or obese. People with binge-eating disorder who are obese are at higher risk for developing cardiovascular disease and high blood pressure. They also experience guilt, shame, and distress about their binge-eating, which can lead to more binge-eating.

How Are Eating Disorders Treated?

Adequate nutrition, reducing excessive exercise, and stopping purging behaviors are the foundations of treatment. Specific forms of psychotherapy, or talk therapy, and medication are effective for many eating disorders. However, in more chronic cases, specific treatments have not yet been identified. Treatment plans often are tailored to individual needs and may include one or more of the following:

- Individual, group, and/or family psychotherapy
- Medical care and monitoring

- Nutritional counseling
- Medications.

Some patients may also need to be hospitalized to treat problems caused by malnutrition or to ensure they eat enough if they are very underweight.

Treating Anorexia Nervosa

Treating anorexia nervosa involves three components:

- Restoring the person to a healthy weight
- Treating the psychological issues related to the eating disorder
- Reducing or eliminating behaviors or thoughts that lead to insufficient eating and preventing relapse.

Some research suggests that the use of medications, such as antidepressants, antipsychotics, or mood stabilizers, may be modestly effective in treating patients with anorexia nervosa. These medications may help resolve mood and anxiety symptoms that often occur along with anorexia nervosa. It is not clear whether antidepressants can prevent some weight-restored patients with anorexia nervosa from relapsing. Although research is still ongoing, no medication yet has shown to be effective in helping someone gain weight to reach a normal level.

Different forms of psychotherapy, including individual, group, and family-based, can help address the psychological reasons for the illness. In a therapy called the Maudsley approach, parents of adolescents with anorexia nervosa assume responsibility for feeding their child. This approach appears to be very effective in helping people gain weight and improve eating habits and moods. Shown to be effective in case studies and clinical trials, the Maudsley approach is discussed in some guidelines and studies for treating eating disorders in younger, nonchronic patients.

Other research has found that a combined approach of medical attention and supportive psychotherapy designed specifically for anorexia nervosa patients is more effective than psychotherapy alone. The effectiveness of a treatment depends on the person

Prevalence of Eating Disorders Among Adolescents

Percentage of adolescents diagnosed at some point in their lifetime with an eating disorder

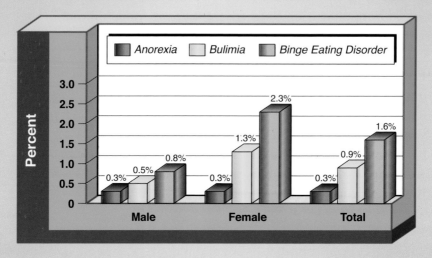

Taken from: Sonja A. Swanson et al., "Prevalence and Correlates of Eating Disorders in Adolescents," *Archives of General Psychiatry*, vol. 68, no. 7, 2011, pp. 714–723.

involved and his or her situation. Unfortunately, no specific psychotherapy appears to be consistently effective for treating adults with anorexia nervosa. However, research into new treatment and prevention approaches is showing some promise. One study suggests that an online intervention program may prevent some at-risk women from developing an eating disorder. Also, specialized treatment of anorexia nervosa may help reduce the risk of death.

Treating Bulimia Nervosa

As with anorexia nervosa, treatment for bulimia nervosa often involves a combination of options and depends upon the needs of the individual. To reduce or eliminate binge-eating and purging behaviors, a patient may undergo nutritional counseling and psychotherapy, especially cognitive behavioral therapy (CBT), or be prescribed medication. CBT helps a person focus on his or her current problems and how to solve them. The therapist helps the patient learn how to identify distorted or unhelpful thinking patterns, recognize, and change inaccurate beliefs, relate to others in more positive ways, and change behaviors accordingly.

CBT that is tailored to treat bulimia nervosa is effective in changing binge-eating and purging behaviors and eating attitudes. Therapy may be individual or group-based.

Some antidepressants, such as fluoxetine (Prozac), which is the only medication approved by the U.S. Food and Drug Administration (FDA) for treating bulimia nervosa, may help patients who also have depression or anxiety. Fluoxetine also appears to help reduce binge-eating and purging behaviors, reduce the chance of relapse, and improve eating attitudes.

Treating Binge-Eating Disorder

Treatment options for binge-eating disorder are similar to those used to treat bulimia nervosa. Psychotherapy, especially CBT that is tailored to the individual, has been shown to be effective. Again, this type of therapy can be offered in an individual or group environment.

Fluoxetine and other antidepressants may reduce binge-eating episodes and help lessen depression in some patients.

How Are Males Affected by Eating Disorders?

Like females who have eating disorders, males also have a distorted sense of body image. For some, their symptoms are similar to those seen in females. Others may have muscle dysmorphia, a type of disorder that is characterized by an extreme concern with becoming more muscular. Unlike girls with eating disorders, who mostly want to lose weight, some boys with muscle dysmorphia see themselves as smaller than they really are and want to gain weight or bulk up. Men and boys are more likely to use steroids or other dangerous drugs to increase muscle mass.

Although males with eating disorders exhibit the same signs and symptoms as females, they are less likely to be diagnosed with what is often considered a female disorder. More research is needed to understand the unique features of these disorders among males.

What Is Being Done to Better Understand and Treat Eating Disorders?

Researchers are finding that eating disorders are caused by a complex interaction of genetic, biological, behavioral, psychological, and social factors. But many questions still need answers. Researchers are using the latest in technology and science to better understand eating disorders.

One approach involves the study of human genes. Researchers are studying various combinations of genes to determine if any DNA variations are linked to the risk of developing eating disorders.

Neuroimaging studies are also providing a better understanding of eating disorders and possible treatments. One study showed different patterns of brain activity between women with bulimia nervosa and healthy women. Using functional magnetic resonance imaging (fMRI), researchers were able to see the differences in brain activity while the women performed a task that involved self-regulation (a task that requires overcoming an automatic or impulsive response).

Psychotherapy interventions are also being studied. One such study of adolescents found that more adolescents with bulimia nervosa recovered after receiving Maudsley model family-based treatment than those receiving supportive psychotherapy that did not specifically address the eating disorder.

Researchers are studying questions about behavior, genetics, and brain function to better understand risk factors, identify biological markers, and develop specific psychotherapies and medications that can target areas in the brain that control eating behavior. Neuroimaging and genetic studies may provide clues for how each person may respond to specific treatments for these medical illnesses.

TWO

Binge Eating Is a Serious Eating Disorder

Sunny Sea Gold

> In the following viewpoint Sunny Sea Gold describes the symptoms of binge eating disorder (BED). Although the illness is not a frequently discussed eating disorder, it impacts more people than anorexia and bulimia combined. The author relates the experiences of several teenagers who have suffered from the eating disorder and emphasizes the importance of seeking treatment. Gold battled with BED as a teenager and is the author of *Food: The Good Girl's Drug*.

When I was sixteen years old, I sold candy bars to raise money for my junior class student council. After carting them around all day at school, I finally gave in to my chocolate craving and had one. Then two. Then three, four, five. Despite feeling sick to my stomach, I couldn't stop. I ate half a dozen 100 Grand candy bars that afternoon, and then spent the evening trying to make myself throw up.

I'd been obsessed with dieting and calories since I was thirteen, and any attempts to resist junk food always ended with me eating stuff by the bag, box, and tub; but after downing those candy bars that day, I knew something was wrong. I didn't have anorex-

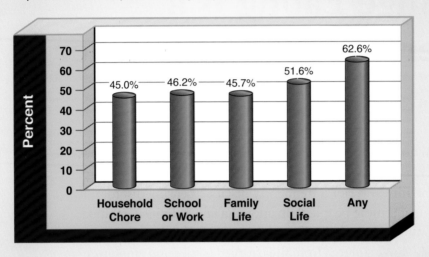

Impacts of Binge Eating Disorder on Adolescents' Daily Life

Percentage of adolescents with binge eating disorder who have experienced an impaired ability to perform roles due to their disorder

Taken from: Sonja A. Swanson et al., "Prevalence and Correlates of Eating Disorders in Adolescents," *Archives of General Psychiatry*, vol. 68, no. 7, 2011, pp. 714–723.

ia, because I wasn't starving myself, and I didn't have bulimia, because I couldn't actually get myself to purge.

It turned out that I had something I had never heard of before: binge eating disorder (BED), an illness characterized by frequent overeating during which you feel out of control and then very upset afterward. And I wasn't the only one suffering from it. Despite the fact that people don't talk about it as much, BED is more common than anorexia and bulimia combined: A study last year [2011] by the National Institute of Mental Health found that 1.6 percent of all American teens have it, compared with 0.3 percent who have anorexia and 0.9 percent who are struggling with bulimia.

Kelsey, a seventeen-year-old from Philadelphia, recently discovered that she's one of the hundreds of thousands of teen girls dealing with BED. "A typical binge will go something like this:

I tell myself I'm only going to have one cookie, but it turns into ten," she says. "After I eat those, I'll grab some chips because I want something salty. Next thing you know, I'm standing in front of the fridge eating leftovers. Then I'll want something sweet again, so I'll have a couple of ice cream sandwiches and some cereal." She confesses that she repeatedly raids the fridge and cupboards although she's not hungry, and even when she's already full. "It's as if I'm on autopilot— just shoving all the food in—and before I realize it, I've eaten a ton," she says. Too ashamed to binge eat in front of others, Kelsey waits until she's home alone: "When my mom leaves, I sometimes go straight to the kitchen so I can have a huge pig-out with no one around."

A Loss of Control

Of course, everyone overeats once in a while—accidentally finishing off a big bag of chips while watching TV or having seconds of pie at Thanksgiving—but binge eaters' behavior goes way beyond that. "The key issue that distinguishes binge eating disorder from the normal overeating we all do is the loss of control, and one sign that there may be a binge eating problem is if it causes distress to the person and interferes with her life in some way," explains Cynthia Bulik, Ph.D., director of the University of North Carolina Eating Disorders Program and author of the book *Crave: Why You Binge Eat and How to Stop*. . . . "This could mean not going out with friends to eat, avoiding social situations, like parties, in which there is food, and choosing to stay at home with your binge foods over going to school or an activity."

For Kelsey, who's currently in her senior year of high school, overeating is definitely getting in the way of her happiness. "I binge eat almost every day and I feel disgusting," she says. "I've gained fifteen pounds in the last few months, and it's a struggle to get out of bed every morning. When I look in the mirror I want to cry. None of my clothes fit anymore, so now I just wear sweatpants and T-shirts to school and no makeup. I've lost all my confidence."

Although Kelsey and other teens with BED hate what they are doing, experts say it's foolish to assume they can simply end the behavior. "Though people might think it's easy for someone to stop binge eating, it's no easier to overcome than anorexia or bulimia," says Ovidio Bermudez, M.D., medical director of Child and Adolescent Services at the Eating Recovery Center in Denver. "Overcoming an eating disorder isn't just a matter of willpower but requires treatment. Eating disorders, including binge eating disorder, are serious mental illnesses with severe physical complications," he stresses. In fact, just as genes can affect a person's risk of developing diabetes or certain types of cancer, some researchers believe that genetics may play a role in BED. One study of overweight individuals found that a person is twice as likely to binge eat if she has a relative with BED, and another reported that if someone in her immediate family had the disorder, she has a 57 percent chance of having it too.

Thanks to a complex mash-up of factors—like genes, individual personality, upbringing, and difficult life events—that could make some people prone to binge eating, the problem can't be fixed simply by learning about good nutrition. In fact, people with binge eating issues can gorge on healthy foods too. "I'd often binge on nuts, granola bars, and whole-wheat bread," says seventeen-year-old Vanessa,* from Seattle, who went to a therapist to help get her BED and poor body image under control. "I remember thinking it was ironic that I was turning healthy things into something extremely unhealthy. One time, I went to several stores and bought bran muffins, pita chips, and other things like that. Even though I couldn't bring myself to buy and eat junk food, I still went on to ingest thousands of calories."

Dieting Is Not the Answer

While not everyone with BED is overweight, all of those extra calories can eventually lead to weight gain for many girls. But dieting isn't the answer either. "I've struggled with food and my weight all my life. When I got to high school, I was sick of feeling fat so I went on a diet and lost a lot of weight," says Kelsey. "I

* Name has been changed.

A young woman eats a piece of cake during a binge. Binge eating is an often-overlooked eating disorder.

weighed 117 pounds at the beginning of junior year—but with all the stress of school and my busy schedule, I started bingeing again and am now at 130 pounds." Dieting not only doesn't fix BED, it may make the eating disorder worse and lead to obesity, warns Amy Jaffe, R.D., a nutrition therapist in Coral Gables, Florida. "There's only so long that we as humans can deprive ourselves; it's against our nature. So the binge usually comes after the diet, or a big binge is what ends the diet. It's a vicious cycle and very hard to stop," she says. Kelsey knows this all too well: "I'll go to school and not eat all day, trying to make up for the binge from the night before, but then I'll end up eating a million calories when I get home," she says.

Indeed, BED is tough to tackle, but it can be conquered. "I've learned so much through therapy and reading books about why my relationship to food was the way it was," says Vanessa. "Overeating was a way for me to lose control and stuff down my feelings." She has also stopped being so strict about what she can and can't eat, which has helped curb her binges. "I let myself eat what I want, healthy or not. So now I don't go out and overeat healthy food when what I'm really craving is little bit of junk," she explains. "I've also educated myself on the vitamins and minerals that are in food. Thinking about how they can help my body instead of focusing on calories has helped me see the big picture and not view food as good or evil."

Seeking the Path to Recovery

Emily, nineteen, from Houston, says she's on the path to recovery after educating herself about BED. "I knew that I didn't like my body and that I snuck food and overate regularly, but I didn't understand that it was a psychological disorder at first," she says. "Finally being able to put a name on something I've struggled with my whole life was the most important step toward getting healthier, both physically and mentally." Emily still binges once in a while, but she doesn't beat herself up about it as much. "I felt more ashamed about it when I didn't know why I was doing it. I used to think I had no self-discipline, which really sucked, because I worked very hard to be the best at everything. Now, I feel more at peace with myself and I don't let frustration and shame overwhelm me when I slip up," she says.

As with Vanessa and Emily, seeing a therapist and reading self-help books helped me figure out what was going on in my relationship with food. Eventually, I completely recovered from BED. If you're worried that you might have a binge eating problem (even if it's not full-blown BED), educating yourself is the first step toward getting better. In addition to checking out books on this topic, learn the basic facts at the Binge Eating Disorder

Association's website (bedaonline.com) and check out support sites, like something-fishy.org and nationaleatingdisorders.org.

Telling someone you trust about your binge eating can be scary, but it's crucial as well. Talk to an adult you trust, whether it's your parent, sports coach, or school counselor, and ask them to put you in touch with a psychologist or eating disorders specialist. Lastly, be willing to accept help when it's offered. "My mom was the one who first noticed my struggles, and I used to push her away," says Kelsey. "Finally, I told her I wanted help, so she called our family doctor, and he referred me to a therapist and nutritionist. Now I'm receiving treatment, and I hope to get better."

THREE

Many Factors Contribute to Eating Disorders

The Center for Eating Disorders at Sheppard Pratt

In the following viewpoint the Center for Eating Disorders at Sheppard Pratt discusses the various causes of eating disorders. Research on disordered eating is evolving, the center maintains, and this has led to a greater understanding of the factors that contribute to the illnesses. The center outlines the following risk factors for eating disorders: genetics, temperament, biology, trauma, coping skill deficits, family life, sociocultural ideals, and dieting. The Center for Eating Disorders at Sheppard Pratt, located in Towson, Maryland, is one of the longest-operating eating disorder treatment facilities in the United States.

Eating disorders include a range of conditions that involve an obsession with food, weight and appearance. The obsession is often so strong that it disrupts an individual's health, social and familial relationships, occupations and daily activities. It is estimated that over 10 million people in the United States suffer from eating disorders such as anorexia, bulimia, and binge eating disorder, and the statistics are growing.

Research on the causes of eating disorders is constantly evolving, and we continue to gain increased insight into risk factors that may contribute to the illness. However, the answers remain multi-factorial, and they reflect a complex combination of biopsychosocial factors that may intersect differently for each person.

Several major risk factors for eating disorders are outlined below.

Genetics

Increasing numbers of family, twin, and adoption research studies have provided compelling evidence to show that genetic factors contribute to a predisposition for eating disorders. In other words, individuals who are born with certain genotypes are at heightened risk for the development of an eating disorder. This also means that eating disorders are heritable. Individuals who have had a family member with an eating disorder are 7–12 times more likely to develop one themselves. Newer research is exploring a possible epigenetic influence on eating disorder development. Epigenetics

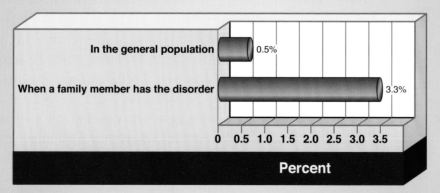

Impact of Genetics on the Development of Eating Disorders

Chance of developing anorexia

In the general population — 0.5%

When a family member has the disorder — 3.3%

0   0.5   1.0   1.5   2.0   2.5   3.0   3.5

Percent

Taken from: Barbara Wexler, "The Influences of Mental Health and Culture on Weight and Eating Disorders," *Weight in America: Obesity, Eating Disorders, and Other Health Risks*. Detroit: Gale, 2013, p. 53.

is a process by which environmental effects alter the way genes are expressed.

Temperament

Some of the genes that have been identified to contribute to eating disorders are associated with specific personality traits. These aspects of personality are thought to be highly heritable and often exist before the eating disorder and can persist after recovery. The following traits are common among people who develop an eating disorder but all of these personality characteristics can exist in the absence of an eating disorder as well.

- obsessive thinking
- perfectionism
- sensitivity to reward and punishment, harm avoidance
- neuroticism (emotional instability and hypersensitivity)
- impulsivity, especially in bulimia nervosa
- rigidity and excessive persistence, especially in anorexia nervosa

Biology

Even in healthy individuals without eating disorders, states of semi-starvation have been shown to trigger obsessive behavior around food, depression, anxiety and neuroticism that promote a continued cycle of starvation. Additionally, brain imaging studies have shown that people with eating disorders may have altered brain circuitry that contributes to eating disorders. Differences in the anterior insula, striatal regions, and anterior ventral striatal pathway have been discovered. Problems with the serotonin pathway have also been discovered. These differences may help to explain why people who develop anorexia nervosa are able to inhibit their appetite, why people who develop binge eating disorder are vulnerable to overeating when they are hungry, and why people who develop bulimia nervosa have less ability to control impulses to purge.

Trauma

Traumatic events such as physical or sexual abuse sometimes precipitate the development of an eating disorder. Victims of trauma often struggle with shame, guilt, body dissatisfaction and a feeling of a lack of control. The eating disorder may become the individual's attempt to regain control or cope with these intense emotions. In some cases, the eating disorder is an expression of self-harm or misdirected self-punishment for the trauma. As many as 50% of those with eating disorders may also be struggling with trauma disorders. It's important to treat both conditions concurrently in a comprehensive and integrated approach which is why The Center for Eating Disorders offers a specialized treatment track for women and men with eating disorders who've also experienced trauma.

Coping Skill Deficits

Individuals with eating disorders are often lacking the skills to tolerate negative experiences. Behaviors such as restricting, purging, bingeing and excessive exercise often develop in response to emotional pain, conflict, low self-esteem, anxiety, depression, stress or trauma. In the absence of more positive coping skills, the eating disorder behaviors may provide acute relief from distress but quickly lead to more physical and psychological harm. Instead of helping, the eating disorder behaviors only serve to maintain a dangerous cycle of emotional dysregulation and numbing feelings. Effective treatment for the eating disorder involves education about and practice of alternative coping mechanisms and self-soothing techniques such as in Dialectic Behavior Therapy.

Family

The family is an integral system in the healthy development of a child and can play an important role in the recovery process. Unfortunately, in the past, parents were often blamed as the sole cause of their child's eating disorder. As more research is done on the diverse contributing factors discussed above, it becomes more and more clear that this is not the case. While stressful or chaotic

Many factors contribute to the development of an eating disorder, but genetic makeup and family dynamics are thought to be two major ones.

family situations may intersect with other triggers to exacerbate or maintain the illness, they do not cause eating disorders. It's also important to note that some family dynamics, which were once assumed to be precursors to an eating disorder, may develop as a response to a family member's struggle with an eating disorder. The Academy of Eating Disorders (AED) recently released a position paper that clarifies the role of the family in the acquisition of eating disorders. The paper points out that there is no data to support the idea that anorexia or bulimia are caused by a certain type of family dynamic or parenting style. Alternatively, there is strong evidence that family-based treatment for younger patients, implemented early on in their illness, leads to positive results and improvements in conjunction with professionally guided family intervention. While parents and families are not to blame for eating disorders, they can play a role in helping kids establish a positive body image, one of the most important protective factors against eating disorders.

Sociocultural Ideals

Our media's increased obsession with the thin-ideal and industry promotion of a "perfect" body may contribute to unrealistic body ideals in people with and without eating disorders. An increase in access to global media and technological advances such as Photoshop and airbrushing have further skewed our perception of attainable beauty standards. In 1998, a researcher documented the response of adolescents in rural Fiji to the introduction of western television. This new media exposure resulted in significant preoccupations related to shape and weight, purging behavior to control weight, and negative body image. This landmark study illustrated a vulnerability to the images and values imported with media. Given that many individuals exposed to media and cultural ideals do not develop clinical eating disorders, it may be that individuals already at-risk, have increased vulnerability to society's messages about weight and beauty and, perhaps, seek out increased exposure to them.

Dieting

Dieting is the most common precipitating factor in the development of an eating disorder. In the U.S., more than $60 billion is spent every year on diets and weight-loss products. Despite dieting's 95–98% failure rate, people continue to buy dangerous products and take extreme measures to lose weight. Restrictive dieting is not effective for weight loss and is an unhealthy behavior for anyone, especially children and adolescents. For individuals who are genetically predisposed to eating disorders, dieting can be the catalyst for heightened obsessions about weight and food. Dieting also intensifies feelings of guilt and shame around food which may ultimately contribute to a cycle of restricting, purging, bingeing or excessive exercise. 9.5 out of 10 people who lose weight through dieting gain back all of their weight within 1–5 years; half of them gain back to a weight that's above their starting weight. More worrisome though is that dieting is associated with higher rates of depression and eating disorders and increased health problems related to weight cycling. Intuitive eating and the health-at-every size paradigms are recommended as alternatives to diets for people looking to improve their health and overall well-being.

FOUR

I Don't Want to Be Told I'm Pretty as I Am. I Want to Live in a World Where That's Irrelevant

Laurie Penny

> In the following viewpoint Laurie Penny argues that the fashion, beauty, and cosmetics industries promote harmful standards of beauty. These industries have no interest in the well-being of women, Penny contends, and they encourage unhealthy eating. Penny believes that these industries exploit existing social prejudice to promote a narrow stereotype of "beauty." Instead of fighting for every woman's right to feel beautiful, the author would like to fight for the right *not* to be pretty. Penny is a contributing editor to the *New Statesman*, a weekly current affairs magazine in Great Britain.

Body image is big business. This spring, the Brazilian modelling agency Star Models has launched a graphic campaign with the intention of showing young women how horrific acute anorexia is. It shows models photoshopped to the proportions of fashion sketches—spindly legs, twig-like arms, wobbling lollipop heads.

A makeup artist prepares a model for the catwalk. Many blame the fashion industry for perpetuating unrealistic concepts of beauty to women.

Given the high-profile deaths of two South American models from anorexia—one of whom, Luisel Ramos, dropped dead of heart failure at a catwalk show—one might interpret this as a way for the agency to detoxify its brand while drumming up a little publicity. But that would be too cynical; the global fashion industry really cares about young women's health now. That's why model agencies were recently discovered recruiting outside Swedish eating disorder clinics.

Elsewhere, a new campaign video by Dove uses facial composite drawing to demonstrate how women underestimate their own looks. Dove is owned by Unilever, a multi-billion-pound company that seems to have little problem using sexism and body fascism to advertise other products: it also manufactures Lynx, of the "fire a bullet at a pretty girl to make her clothes fall off" campaign, the Slim-Fast fake food range, and more than one brand of the bleach sold to women of colour to burn their skin "whiter".

The fashion, beauty and cosmetics industries have no interest in improving women's body image. Playing on women's insecurities to create a buzz and push products is an old trick but there's a cynical new trend in advertising that peddles distressing stereotypes with one hand and ways to combat that distress with the other. We're not like all the rest, it whispers. We think you're pretty just as you are. Now buy our skin grease and smile. The message, either way, is that before we can be happy, women have to feel "beautiful", which preferably starts with being "beautiful".

Let's get one thing straight: women don't develop eating disorders, self-harm and have other issues with our body image because we're stupid. Beauty and body fascism aren't just in our heads— they affect our lives every day, whatever our age, whatever we look like, and not just when we happen to open a glossy magazine.

We love to talk, as a society, about beauty and body weight— indeed, many women writers are encouraged to talk about little else. What we seldom mention are the basic, punishing double standards of physical appearance that are used to keep women of all ages and backgrounds in our place. For a bloke, putting on a half-decent suit and shaving with a new razor is enough to count as "making an effort". For women, it's an expensive, time-consuming and painful rigamarole of cutting, bleaching, dyeing, shaving, plucking, starving, exercising and picking out clothes that send the right message without making you look like a shop-window dress-up dolly.

Eating disorders such as anorexia and bulimia are severe mental illnesses but they exist at the extreme end of a scale of trauma in which millions of women and girls struggle for much of their lives. The fashion, diet and beauty industries exploit and exaggerate existing social prejudice, encouraging women to starve ourselves, to burn time and money and energy in a frantic, self-defeating struggle to resemble a stereotype of "beauty" that is narrowing every year.

Studies have shown that, across the pay grades, women who weigh less are paid more for the same work and have a better chance of promotion than those who are heavier. In politics, in business and in the arts, accomplished and powerful men are free to get fat and sloppy, but women can expect to be judged for

The Impact of Weight on Earnings by Gender

Predicted annual wages/salary (2008 US$)

Taken from: Timothy A. Judge and Daniel M. Cable, "When It Comes to Pay, Do the Thin Win? The Effect of Weight on Pay for Men and Women," *Journal of Applied Psychology*, vol. 96, no. 1, January 2011, p. 14.

their looks if they dare to have a high-profile job: we're either too unattractive to be tolerated or too pretty to have anything worth saying. Beauty is about class, money, power and privilege—and it always has been. Women and girls are taught that being thin and pretty is the only sure way to get ahead in life, even though this is manifestly not the case.

Those few young women who have fought their way to public acclaim despite lacking the proportions of catwalk models are expected to account for themselves in interviews, from the Oscar-winning singer Adele to the only-ever-so-slightly-plump Lena Dunham.

It's hard to feel all right about yourself in this sort of toxic beauty culture: as long as "fat" is the worst thing you can possibly call a woman, any of us who dares to speak up or out about what is happening will be called fat, whether or not we are.

"Fat" is subjective and socially situated, and it's the slur most commonly directed at any girl or woman who asserts herself, whether physically or politically. Even the most stereotypically thin and beautiful woman will find herself dismissed as unattractive if what comes out of her mouth happens to threaten male privilege, which is why feminists of all stripes continue to be labelled "fat and ugly". This culture would still prefer women to take up as little space as possible.

Rather than fighting for every woman's right to feel beautiful, I would like to see the return of a kind of feminism that tells women and girls everywhere that maybe it's all right not to be pretty and perfectly well behaved. That maybe women who are plain, or large, or old, or differently abled, or who simply don't give a damn what they look like because they're too busy saving the world or rearranging their sock drawer, have as much right to take up space as anyone else.

I think if we want to take care of the next generation of girls we should reassure them that power, strength and character are more important than beauty and always will be, and that even if they aren't thin and pretty, they are still worthy of respect. That feeling is the birthright of men everywhere. It's about time we claimed it for ourselves.

FIVE

Social Media Can Trigger or Worsen Eating Disorders

Iris Mansour

> In the following viewpoint Iris Mansour discusses the relationship between the Internet and disordered eating. She reports on pro-anorexia and pro-bulimia websites as well as the rise of "thinspiration," which celebrates extreme thinness with inspirational messages and faux-nutritional advice. The author writes that social media sites offer havens for eating disorder communities, allowing people suffering from these illnesses to experience validation from anonymous users online. Mansour is a British journalist who has written for *Fortune*, Reuters, *Quartz*, *The Guardian*, and *Time Out*.

Rachel Cowey calls her illness "Ursula." It helped to picture an enemy, the witch in *The Little Mermaid* who manipulates Ariel into giving up her voice.

The eating disorder had ravaged her body, leaving her with osteoporosis at 19. Cowey stares into the shaky camera in her bedroom. "I am not anorexia. I am Rachel," she declares, as if staring Ursula square in the eye.

She's broadcasting on the Team Recovery YouTube channel . . . where Cowey and cofounders Sarah Robertson and Ali

McPherson discuss the lows of battling an eating disorder and the highs of recovering from one.

The three women conceptualized Team Recovery after confronting the overwhelming mountain of online content that worships extreme thinness.

In recent years, the web has exploded with images, blogs and microsites that glorify dangerous weight loss at any cost. Photos of emaciated girls tagged with #thinspiration and #thinspo saturate Twitter feeds and Tumblrs. Waist-down shots picture girls in gym gear that hangs off their shrinking bodies. Pinterest photos depict women with #thighgap; they're so thin that, even with feet

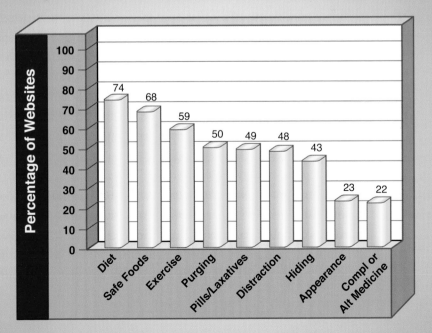

Analyzing the Content of Pro–Eating Disorder Websites

Percentages of websites featuring various tips for engaging in eating-disordered behaviors

Taken from: Dina L. G. Borzekowski et al., "e-Ana and e-Mia: A Content Analysis of Pro–Eating Disorder Websites," *American Journal of Public Health*, vol. 100, no. 8, August 2010, pp. 1526–1534.

together, their thighs don't touch, a genetic impossibility in most, but one that can occur in the dangerously thin.

The Rise of Thinspiration

In a sense, the phenomenon is nothing new. Similar photos have been online since the late '90s. But their volume and accessibility is unprecedented. One survey shows that between 2006 and 2008 alone, the number of such sites had increased by 470%. At the same time, dieters are getting younger. According to NEDA, 40–60% of girls aged 6–12 are concerned about their weight or about becoming too fat.

Yet for Cowey, the Internet was the only option for positive outreach.

Pro-anorexia and pro-bulimia sites have existed since the dawn of the Internet. Experts use the terms "pro-ana" and "pro-mia" to describe the type of online content that glorifies treacherously thin bodies, implies eating disorders or, in some cases, even directly advocates starving or purging.

In the mid-2000s these sites were vilified for their content: photos of emaciated bodies and tips on how to achieve them. The images were and continue to be particularly dangerous. If you're at risk of an eating disorder, they can trigger and fuel a devastating psychological illness that manifests in body and mind.

Today's social media has upped the stakes. With blogging platforms like Tumblr, web users no longer require coding knowledge to publish a website. With micro-blogging, sharing images is easier than ever.

"It's taken on a whole new life," says Claire Mysko, project consultant for the National Eating Disorder Association (NEDA). "Now they're everywhere you turn. There are entire sites and hashtags devoted to these types of images."

Thinspiration bears similarities to early pro-ana sites. At its core it celebrates extreme thinness. But unlike the first sites, thinspiration is couched with motivational quotes, like "Keep Calm and Thighgap On," alongside faux-nutritional advice.

In this way, thinspiration has mirrored a cultural evolution. As society became more interested in health and fitness, pro-ana messages latched onto the trend like a parasite to its host.

Don't miss the underlying message, though: "Being emaciated will make you happy."

It isn't entirely the Internet's fault. "I don't want to blame thinspiration for the epidemic, because we were already in it," says Margo Maine, Ph.D., who's been treating eating disorders for almost 35 years. "In our culture for women, being thin is still seen as pinnacle as success," says Maine. She points out the irony: We stigmatize the extremes like anorexia and bulimia, but "they are just one step ahead of us."

The Dangers of Thinspiration

Early pro-ana forums were explicit in their goal: weight loss at all costs. But today's thinspiration messages are blurred, which experts believe makes them all the more dangerous.

While social media can be a positive place for eating disorder sufferers, it can also provide negative reinforcement and glamorization of dangerous eating habits.

Maine explains, "Instead of looking at eating disorder habits as a pathology, thinspiration treats them as a lifestyle choice."

Posts about self-harm, depression and even suicide frequently show up on thinspiration feeds. "It's characterized as this dark world, which it is," says Mysko. "But it's posted by people who are really struggling. They're not villains; they're people who are in a really bad place and need help."

"To think that 10 years ago it was only some web forums, and now it's just everywhere, is really scary," says Cowey via Skype, from her home in Northern England.

Cowey logged on to pro-ana forums from 10 P.M. until 4 A.M. "With an eating disorder your body stays awake longer because it's searching for food, so I used to be awake until about four in the morning on the pro-ana websites," she says.

She used a pro-ana quote as her MSN tagline: "We turn skeletons into goddess so that they might teach us not to need." She saved pictures of emaciated girls on her computer, including one of model Kate Moss with jutting ribs.

"If I ever wanted to eat, I'd look at these pictures and remind myself what I wanted to look like," says Cowey. . . .

Social Media Spurs Competition Among Anorexics

Marissa (last name withheld) began to develop anorexic tendencies in 2002, and bulimia in 2003. Shortly after, she found Facebook.

"My eating disorder took off like a rocket," she says. Marissa, 27, would log on as soon as she woke up and take a quick scan of her News Feed. Among the typical high school posts, she found images of girls so thin their bones stuck out, status updates that read "going back to treatment," wall posts detailing number of pounds lost and number of pounds gained. Once or twice she even caught an image of a girl in a hospital bed, a feeding tube in her mouth.

Maine explains, "Eating disorders have always been a competitive sport, but social media just increases the number of people you are competing with." This is especially true of anorexia. Marissa says, "A very big part of the eating disorder is competition of 'who's the thinnest, who's the best at it, who's the sickest.'"

With Facebook, "you had competition at your fingertips all the time," she says.

She explains that in analog world if you were anorexic you might have been in competition with four other girls at school, whose bodies and damaged health you would have seen with your own eyes. Online, however, there's no way of knowing what's doctored and what's real.

There was no respite. At midday Marissa would log on to Facebook again. Much in the same way you'd check in on your favorite blog, she carried a mental list of friends she'd met in treatment. She would scour their profiles for new photos.

"I was obsessive," Marissa says. "I wanted to see if I was thinner than them. If I was, that was great. If I wasn't, that was a catastrophe," one that led her to restrict her food and lose even more weight.

After meeting people at treatment centers, they'd form Facebook groups. People would share information about recent visits to the hospital and numbers from their latest weigh-ins.

"It developed into an eating disorder culture," she says, "where it not only seemed normal, but it was kind of a community of people who were not getting well."

Receiving Validation Online

The anonymity of the web lets people suffering from an already private illness keep their binging, purging or starving hidden from family and friends, all the while experiencing validation from anonymous users online.

Marissa looked at these wall-to-wall photos in private. Cocooning herself in her room with her laptop made for a more intimate yet lonely experience.

"Nobody knew I was doing it. I didn't tell anyone. I didn't even tell my therapist," she says. If you're with a friend and thinspiration-worthy images come up in a magazine or on TV, there's a strong chance they'll jump and comment that you can't be that weight and be healthy. But on pro-ana sites, where the majority of users have disordered eating—otherwise they wouldn't be there—few offer a voice of reason.

It was only when Marissa went away to a residential unit for a year and a half, where she couldn't go online without a counselor, and Facebook use was forbidden entirely, that she was able to sustain a period of recovery. By the time she got home, the cycle was broken and she'd developed goals beyond calorie-consumption.

Website Bans Won't Solve the Problem

Facebook employs stringent community guidelines regarding pro-ed content. If someone posts images or text that suggests self-abuse, users are expected to report the activity. Facebook employees then review every piece of content and decide whether it should be removed. Sometimes Facebook may also take extra steps to get in touch with users who are showing extreme behavior and need help.

Pinterest also prohibits posts promoting self-harm. The company has worked with NEDA to develop a list of search terms that prompt a warning and include help resources. Generally, moderators don't ban topics altogether, because someone searching for "warning signs," "help," "support groups" or "recovery stories" may include the term in his or her searches. It's a similar story for Tumblr.

"You have to view the Internet as a neutral tool that can be used either for positive or negative purposes," says Sharon Hodgson, who founded one of the earliest pro-recovery forums, We Bite Back.

Hodgson says banning websites is pointless and misguided; it misses what these sites, feeds and Pinterest boards really amount to. "It's not a website, it's not a hashtag. It's a community," she says. "You'll have people finding each other through the hashtags just as they've used many other mechanisms to do so in the last two decades."

SIX

Is Anorexia a Cultural Disease?

Carrie Arnold

> In the following viewpoint Carrie Arnold argues that eating disorders are not a cultural phenomenon. Eating disorders have various causes, she maintains, and focusing on cultural causes ignores the multifaceted nature of these disorders. The author believes the distorted view of eating disorders has limited the amount of research funding and made it difficult to develop new treatments. Arnold is a science writer and the author of *Decoding Anorexia: How Breakthroughs in Science Offer Hope for Eating Disorders.*

From the outside, my eating disorder looked a lot like vanity run amok. It looked like a diet or an obsession with the size of my thighs. I spewed self- and body-hatred to friends and family for well over a decade. Anorexia may have looked like a disorder brought about by the fashion industry, by a desire to be thin and model-perfect that got out of hand.

Except that it wasn't. I wasn't being vain when I craned my neck trying to check out my butt in the mirror—I truly had no idea what size I was anymore. I was so afraid of calories that I refused to use lip balm and, at one point, was unable to drink water. I was terrified of gaining weight, but I couldn't explain why.

As I lay in yet another hospital bed hooked up to yet another set of IVs and heart monitors, the idea of eating disorders as a cultural disorder struck me as utterly ludicrous. I didn't read fashion magazines, and altering my appearance wasn't what drove me to start restricting my food intake. I just wanted to feel better; I thought cutting out snacks might be a good way to make that happen. The more I read, the more I came to understand that culture is only a small part of an eating disorder. Much of my eating disorder, I learned, was driven by my own history of anxiety and depression, by my tendency to focus on the details at the expense of the big picture, and by hunger circuits gone awry. The overwhelming amount of misinformation about eating disorders—what they are and what causes them—drove me to write my latest book, *Decoding Anorexia: How Breakthroughs in Science Offer Hope for Eating Disorders*.

Eating Disorders Have Various Causes

Efforts to fight eating disorders still target cultural phenomena, especially images of overly thin, digitally altered models. Last month [August 2012], the Academy for Eating Disorders [AED] and the Binge Eating Disorder Association [BEDA] issued a press release condemning the high-end department store Barneys for giving beloved Disney characters a makeover. Minnie Mouse and Daisy Duck were stretched like taffy to appear emaciated in honor of Barneys' holiday ad campaign. The eating disorders groups wrote:

> Viewership of such images is associated with low self-esteem and body dissatisfaction in young girls and women, placing them at risk for development of body image disturbances and eating disorders. These conditions can have devastating psychological as well as medical consequences. This campaign runs counter to efforts across the globe to improve both the health of runway models and the representation of body image by the fashion industry.

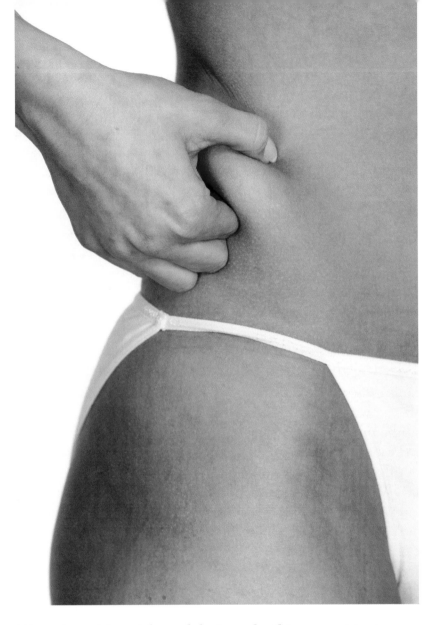

Obsession with weight and desire to be thin are not just reactions to cultural ideas of beauty; often eating disorders can come from genetic factors or past trauma.

All of which is technically true. But when you look at the research literature, several studies indicate that environmental factors such as emaciated models are actually a minor factor in what puts people at risk of an eating disorder. A 2000 study published in the *American Journal of Psychiatry* found that about 60 percent (and up to 85 percent) of a person's risk for developing anorexia was due to genetics. A 2006 follow-up study in the *Archives of General Psychiatry* found that only 5 percent of a person's risk of developing anorexia came from shared environmental factors like models and magazine culture. A far greater environmental risk (which the study estimated constituted 35 percent of someone's risk of anorexia) came from what researchers call non-shared environmental factors, which are unique to each individual, such as being bullied on the playground or being infected with a bacterium like *Streptococcus*. (Several very small studies have linked the sudden onset of anorexia and obsessive-compulsive symptoms to an autoimmune reaction to strep infections.)

Fighting the Eating Disorder Stereotype

Eating disorders existed long before the advent of supermodels. Researchers believe the "starving saints" of the Middle Ages, like Catherine of Siena, had anorexia. Reports from ancient history indicate that wealthy Romans would force themselves to vomit during feasts, to make room in their stomachs for yet another course. In modern times, anorexia has been reported in rural Africa and in Amish and Mennonite communities, none of which are inundated with images of overly thin women. Nor does culture explain the fact that all Americans are bombarded with these images but only a very tiny portion ever develop a clinical eating disorder.

Frankly, I think the Barneys' creation of Skinny Minnie and her newly svelte compatriots is ridiculous. They look absurd and freakish. I think we should be aware of and speak out against the thin body ideal, the sexualization of children, and the use of digitally altered images in advertising. I think we should do this regardless of the link to eating disorders. My objection to the AED and BEDA's response is that it reinforces an "I wanna look like a model" model for how we think of eating disorders. It implies that eating disorders are seen as issues for white, upper-class women, which means that these life-threatening disorders often go undetected and untreated in men, the poor, and minorities.

The Impact of Limited Research Funding

How sufferers, their families, and our culture at large think about eating disorders sets the agenda for treatment, research, and funding. Until a 2008 lawsuit in New Jersey established that anorexia and bulimia were biologically based mental illnesses, it was legal for insurance companies to deny necessary and lifesaving care. The message to sufferers? *You're not that bad off. You're just making this up. Get over it.*

Too many people can't. Eating disorders have the highest mortality rate of all psychiatric illnesses. Up to 1 in 5 chronic anorexia sufferers will die as a direct result of their illness. Recovery from anorexia is typically thought of as the rule of thirds: One-third of sufferers get better, one-third have periods of recovery interrupted by relapse, and one-third remain chronically ill or die.

Mental Disorder Prevalence vs. Funding

Despite the prevalence of eating disorders, they continue to receive inadequate research funding.

Illness	Prevalence	NIH Research Funds (2011)
Alzheimer's Disease	5.1 million	$450,000,000
Autism	3.6 million	$160,000,000
Schizophrenia	3.4 million	$276,000,000
Eating Disorders	30 million	$28,000,000

Taken from: "Get the Facts on Eating Disorders," National Eating Disorders Association. www.nationaleatingdisorders.org.

Although research into eating disorders is improving, it is still dramatically underfunded compared to other neuropsychiatric conditions. The National Institute of Mental Health estimates that 4.4 percent of the U.S. population, or about 13 million Americans, currently suffers from an eating disorder, and eating disorders receive about $27 million in research funding from the government. That's about $2 per affected person, for a disease that costs the economy billions of dollars in treatment costs and loss of productivity. Schizophrenia, in comparison, receives $110 per affected person in research funding.

The lack of research funding means that it's been difficult to develop new treatments for eating disorders and test them in clinical trials. Several types of psychotherapy have been found effective in the treatment of bulimia and binge-eating disorder, although many sufferers have difficulty maintaining recovery even with state-of-the-art treatment. Thus far, no therapies have been clinically proven for adults with anorexia. Because many of those with anorexia are scared of the idea of eating more and gaining weight, they tend to be reluctant to show up for treatment and follow through with a clinical trial. Researchers have found a type of treatment known as family-based treatment, which uses the family as an ally in fighting their child's eating disorder, to be effective in children, teens, and young adults with anorexia or bulimia.

The message from AED and BEDA is technically correct: More and more children are dieting, whether in response to thin models, obesity prevention efforts, or both. Dieting is potentially dangerous because food restriction can set off a chain of events in a vulnerable person's brain and body. For most people, diets end after a modest weight loss (and are, more often than not, followed by a regain of the lost weight, plus a few "bonus" pounds as a reward for playing). For the 1 percent to 5 percent of the population that has a genetic vulnerability to an eating disorder, that innocent attempt at weight loss, "healthy eating," or other situation that results in fewer calories being eaten than necessary, can trigger a life-threatening eating disorder.

However, focusing on purported cultural "causes" of eating disorders leaves out the much bigger, more multifaceted picture of what these disorders are. Eating disorders result from a complex interplay between genes and environment; it's not *just* culture. Yet most media coverage of eating disorders focuses on these types of cultural factors. Well over half of the eating disorder stories I see are about celebrities. Celebrities suffer from eating disorders, too, but they are a small fraction of the total number of sufferers out there. Eating disorders aren't solely about wanting to be thin. They aren't about celebrity culture or the supermodel *du jour*. They are real illnesses that ruin lives.

SEVEN

Eating Disorders Do Not Just Affect "Skinny White Affluent Girls"

Elizabeth Licorish

In the following viewpoint Elizabeth Licorish contends that many people believe disordered eating only impacts skinny white affluent girls (or SWAG). Eating disorders are not a lifestyle choice, the author argues, and they affect people from all races and economic classes. By focusing on the SWAG stereotype, she maintains, society isolates a community of people who suffer from eating disorders and hinders their ability to receive treatment. Licorish is a writer from Philadelphia.

I remember the day [actress] Brittany Murphy died.

I was at my favorite coffee shop, sipping a non-fat, no-whip latte: my liquid lunch.

My mother called as soon as the terrible news exploded my Facebook feed. "Did you *hear* about Brittany Murphy? Did you *see* her latest pictures? She looks *terrible*. She *definitely* had an eating disorder."

See?

See, Elizabeth?

This is what happens.

My mother meant well. I have an abysmal history with food. When I was 21, I weighed 58 pounds and, instead of committing me to another round of inpatient eating disorder treatment, my hopeless, powerless, frustrated friends and family resigned to watch me die. Years later, sipping thin coffee, spinning food porn for a graduate writing workshop, even though I looked normal, I still had lots of issues. I probably always will.

"Let Brittany Murphy be warning to her," my mother probably thought. She phoned that afternoon for the same reason she plays Karen Carpenter carols whenever we bake cookies on Christmas Eve.

What my mother probably didn't realize is my life was as tenuous at 58 pounds as it was during times I weighed twice as much.

A few days ago, I woke up, checked the scale, checked the news. I was surprised to read the latest development in the death of Brittany Murphy: the alleged, lethal levels of toxic, heavy metals detected in her hair, which, apparently, no one thought to test before now. Though these toxicology results have since largely been discredited, it's still too easy to believe Murphy, whose husband passed under eerily similar circumstances, died of pneumonia and iron deficiency anemia, as her death certificate asserts. Because that's how people with eating disorders die.

People with Eating Disorders
Skinny
White
Affluent
Girls

I grew up loving Brittany Murphy's Tai [character in the film *Clueless*]: short, frumpy, sensitive—like me. The fact that Tai is ultimately adorable encouraged me to believe I was lovable too. But Brittany Murphy did not look like Tai when she died. She'd slimmed considerably in the years following her breakout role. Her last photographs show lined biceps, grape eyes. There is, of course, concern over the credibility of this latest toxicology test, especially its administrator's quick conclusion that heavy metals in Murphy's hair suggest murder. Her death may always remain a mystery. But it's possible, it's likely, that Murphy's mainstream image as a thin, rich, white girl—fragile and defenseless by default—masked whatever was *really* wrong with her, whether that thing was criminal, heavy metal exposure, or something less sinister.

The day after the Brittany Murphy announcement, a good friend posted this "article" to my Facebook wall. She was hoping to hear my perspective on "5 Reasons to Date a Girl with an Eating Disorder" [a blog entry by "Tuthmosis" on the Return of Kings website]. An old-fashioned Internet fight ensued. Our mutual Facebook friends had at it, first over whether the piece was supposed to be tongue-in-cheek, then over whether its tone even mattered at all. . . .

I sat back, in virtual silence, content to let the Internet argument resolve itself. Until someone shared this:

"I've unintentionally dated plenty of girls with eating disorders. And in my experience, with the exception of #4, that list is spot on 99% of the time."

I returned to "5 Reasons to Date a Girl with an Eating Disorder," studied its sad stock photography:

"Skinny, Fancy, White Girl, Hunches over Toilet with Index Finger Down Throat"

"Skinny White Girl Sees Fat White Girl Reflected in Mirror"

"Skinny White Girl in Snuggly Underpants and Matching Camisole Cries on Top of Scale"

I couldn't care less what some silly Internet troll says about people with eating disorders.

It deeply disturbs me to realize people actually *believe* these stereotypes.

Eating Disorders Are Considered a Luxury

It hurts to consider this against what might be a tragic oversight in the case of Brittany Murphy, a stereotypical SWAG picture of

Hollywood glamorizes images of skinny, white, affluent girls, but not all women with eating disorders fit that stereotype.

American Disordered Eating, who may not have had an eating disorder at all, whose death is still, ultimately unsolved.

It breaks my heart to remember all the faces I met through 10 years in and out of various eating disorder treatment facilities. They're not all SWAG faces. Some of the most tortured belong to men. Many belong to men and women who are morbidly obese, who are just as depressed and close to death as the most

Impact of Stereotypes on Eating Disorder Treatment

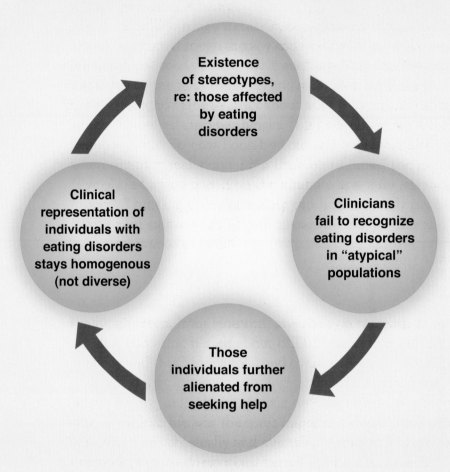

Taken from: Saren, "Who Gets Treatment? Your Ethnicity Matters," *Science of Eating Disorders* (blog), June 1, 2012.

desperate anorexics. The faces in my memories are not all peaches and cream. They're also maple, chestnut, and terra. Many of them are etched with wrinkles. Many are missing teeth.

Tuthmosis writes, "Nothing screams white-girl problems louder than a good old-fashioned eating disorder. But they're more than that. Eating disorders have been—quite appropriately—declared a luxury reserved for only the most privileged members of the female race."

The SWAG Stereotype Is Harmful

The fact that there is no female "race" aside, Tuthmosis a
apparently grew up in the same subculture, which insists
eating disorder is a skinny, rich, white girl disease and, thus,
really a disease at all, but a lifestyle choice for spoiled brats and
body-obsessed neurotics. That eating disorders are so perceptu-
ally linked to affluence is probably why they're so impossible to
treat. It costs upwards of $2,000 a day for eating disorder sufferers
to receive inpatient treatment. Insurance coverage is sparse and
notorious for cutting out before patients make any real progress.
Many, many times I witnessed the sheer horror on people's faces
when they learn they're being discharged because their insurance
is up. I've heard them beg and plead to stay, threaten to take
their own lives, because they can't possibly survive on the outside.
Twenty percent of people with eating disorders *don't* survive on
the outside. It takes, on average, seven years for those who do
survive to recover. And "recover" is such a devastatingly relative
word.

The worst side-effect of the SWAG stereotype is this: the longer we believe only skinny, white, affluent girls suffer from eating
disorders, the more we isolate an entire community of not-skinny,
not-white, not-rich, not-so-young, decidedly-not-female human
beings, who suffer, not only with the soul-sucking burden that is
an eating disorder, but with the belief they can't possible "have"
what's killing them. The risk is it will kill them. And then everyone will wonder why.

Athletes Are Especially Susceptible to Eating Disorders

Gail Hanson-Mayer

In the following viewpoint Gail Hanson-Mayer maintains that athletes are more vulnerable to eating disorders than the average person. She says this likelihood stems from the tendency of some athletes to overexercise and the importance of weight in many sports. The author details the symptoms of common eating disorders that impact athletes and emphasizes the importance of early treatment. Hanson-Mayer is an advanced practice nurse at Walden Behavioral Care in Waltham, Massachusetts, who has worked with athletes who suffer from eating disorders.

You would think that professional athletes, who need to be in near-perfect shape to compete, would be the last people to have an eating disorder. Yet athletes, both men and women, may be two to three times more likely to have an eating disorder than the average person, according to a 1999 study of college athletes by the National Collegiate Athletic Association. A 2004 study of top athletes in Norway reached a similar conclusion, finding that 13.5% of athletes surveyed had an eating disorder, compared with 4.6% of the control group.

Athletes Are Vulnerable to Eating Disorders

As a professional athlete, you may not think these studies apply to you. While additional research is needed, the same characteristics that make college athletes vulnerable to eating disorders may be even more prevalent in professional athletes. At the professional level, the stakes are higher, and the characteristics that help athletes at the highest levels to excel may also be found in those with eating disorders.

A study comparing the psychological profiles of athletes with those of anorexics found many common traits, including high self-expectations, perfectionism, competitiveness, hyperactivity, repetitive exercise routines, compulsiveness, drive, a distorted body image, preoccupation with weight and dieting, and a tendency toward depression.

Professional athletes typically begin training at an early age and are prone to over-exercise. Their parents are sometimes demanding and controlling. Depending on the sport, training may take place in near social isolation.

Athletes are also sometimes obsessive about their weight, because in some sports, being a few pounds lighter or a few pounds heavier can make athletes more competitive. In some cases, they need to stay within a certain weight range to stay in their current weight class.

All of these factors can contribute to the development of an eating disorder. There have been few reports of professional athletes with eating disorders, but that's understandable. For an athlete to admit that he or she has an eating disorder would be about as helpful to a career as admitting to taking anabolic steroids.

There have, however, been plenty of stories about Olympic athletes with eating disorders. Bahne Rabe, a male rower who won eight gold medals, and gymnasts Helga Brathen and Christy Henrich are among those who died from complications related to anorexia. Cathy Rigby, the first American woman to win a medal in World Gymnastics, and Nadia Comaneci, who won nine gold medals, both suffered from bulimia. Comaneci also overcame anorexia.

All Athletes Are at Risk

Women are more likely to develop eating disorders than men, and athletes in sports where body aesthetics or weight are important are more likely to develop eating disorders than those in other sports. Two studies of college athletes, one in 1999 by Craig Johnson of the Laureate Psychiatric Clinic and Hospital in Tulsa and another in 2002 by Katherine Beals of the University of Utah in Salt Lake City, separately found that at least one-third of female college athletes have some type of disordered eating.

However, there are also plenty of male athletes with eating disorders. The National Eating Disorders Association estimates that 33% of male athletes in aesthetic sports (bodybuilding, gymnastics, swimming) and weight-class sports (wrestling, rowing) are affected by eating disorders.

Writing about eating disorders in male athletes in *Sports Medicine* in 2006, Antonia Baum, M.D., of Fairfax Hospital in Falls Church, VA, detailed the extremes that male athletes sometimes go to when weight is a factor in performance. Jockeys may sit in a heated car wearing a rubber suit, use hot-box saunas, self-induce vomiting, or take cocaine and amphetamines to suppress their appetite. Wrestlers abuse diuretics, binge and purge, and take laxatives to make their weight requirements before a match, and then they routinely binge following a match. Crew athletes wear many layers of clothing during runs on hot days to lose weight.

What about male athletes in major sports like baseball, football, and basketball? Anyone can have an eating disorder. *Newsweek* reported that 40% of Cornell University football players surveyed engaged in binging and purging, which is associated with bulimia.

Writing about eating disorders in male athletes, Dr. Baum made a connection between eating disorders and the use of anabolic steroids in football, baseball, and bodybuilding. The use of steroids is a sign of "muscle dysmorphia," where the athlete becomes preoccupied with increasing muscle mass to the exclusion of almost everything else. In addition, athletes who take steroids to improve performance eat more as a result and then try to control their weight, which can result in an eating disorder.

Prevalence of Eating Disorders Between Athletes and Nonathletes

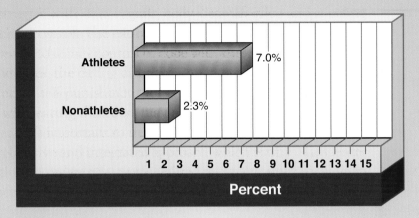

Prevalence of Eating Disorders Between Male and Female Athletes

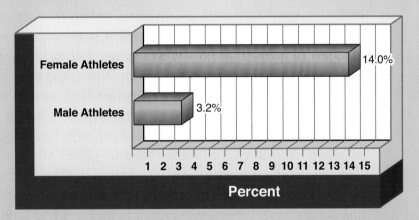

Taken from: Marianne Martinsen and Jorunn Sundgot-Borgen, "Higher Prevalence of Eating Disorders Among Adolescent Elite Athletes than Controls," *Medicine and Science in Sports and Exercise*, vol. 45, no. 6, June 2013, pp. 1188–1197.

While bans on the use of performance-enhancing drugs are being increasingly enforced, the personality traits that lead to their use will still be there, even if steroid use is eliminated from professional sports.

Common Eating Disorders Among Athletes

To determine whether you have, or are in danger of developing, an eating disorder, it helps to have an understanding of the different types of disorders.

The most well-known eating disorder is anorexia nervosa, in which individuals take extreme measures to avoid eating. They have a distorted image of their body and continue to diet, even when they are severely underweight. Other signs include social withdrawal and emotional changes. Few athletes, other than gymnasts, jockeys, runners, and rowers, are likely to develop anorexia.

It is estimated that as many as 33 percent of male athletes, particularly in weight-focused sports like wrestling, struggle with eating disorders.

They could not survive training or competing for long without eating properly. A football lineman would never have anorexia, but could have binge-eating disorder, which is characterized by uncontrollable, excessive eating, followed by feelings of shame and guilt. It is the most common eating disorder, but it is rare among athletes.

The most likely eating disorder for most professional athletes to develop is bulimia nervosa. Those with bulimia typically "binge and purge." Purging is forced vomiting, but some with bulimia may compensate for binging in other ways, such as excessive exercise, or use of laxatives or diet pills. Those who have bulimia can often hide the disorder for years.

Athletes may also be susceptible to muscle dysmorphia, also known as bigorexia, or orthorexia, an obsession with healthy eating.

Those with eating disorders are more apt to have other psychiatric disorders and they have a higher incidence of substance abuse than the general population.

Eating disorders are life-threatening; in fact, they have the highest mortality rate of any psychiatric disorder. At the very least, they can hamper an athlete's performance and make the athlete more susceptible to injuries, like bone fractures. Many athletes have ruined their careers by developing eating disorders and not treating them.

The Importance of Early Treatment

Whether or not you have signs of an eating disorder, consider consulting a nutritionist for help in developing a healthy diet. Many professional teams have nutritionists on staff for that purpose.

If you are binging and purging, or showing other signs of having an eating disorder, you should seek medical help immediately. Especially in the early stages, most people who have an eating disorder are in denial about it. The typical rationalization is, "I'm just doing this to get myself in better shape to play." Failure to accept the problem and do something about it will only lead to bigger problems in the future.

The earlier an eating disorder is treated, the more likely you will be to make a full recovery. You will miss playing time, as your body will need time to heal and your pattern of exercise will need to be disrupted, but failure to act quickly can end your career and can even be a fatal mistake.

NINE

Eating Disorders Do Not Discriminate Based on Sexuality or Gender Identity

Valerie Kusler

In the following viewpoint Valerie Kusler explores the relationship between sexuality and eating disorders. The author finds that lesbian, gay, bisexual, and transgender (LGBT) adolescents are at risk for eating disorders, as they often struggle with accepting their identity and may feel pressures that lead to increased self-doubt, shame, and depression. She dispels common stereotypes about sexuality and eating disorders and maintains that research on eating disorders among people who identify as LGBT is continuing to evolve. Kusler is a therapist at The Ranch, a treatment center near Nashville, Tennessee, that helps women recovering from eating disorders, addiction, mental health issues, and trauma.

October [2011] is LGBT history month, and as the resident eating disorders geek here at Adios Barbie . . . it got me thinking about how little I know about the connection between eating disorders and LGBT population. The default assumptions I've heard are that eating disorders (EDs) are more common in gay males than straight males due to increased pressure to be thin and attractive in the gay community, while lesbians have *fewer* eating disorders than straight women, since they apparently eschew our society's narrow beauty standards. How much truth, if any, is behind these stereotypical assumptions? *Is there a connection or correlation between sexual orientation/gender identity and eating disorders?*

LGBT Adolescents Are at Risk for Eating Disorders

I recently attended the NEDA (National Eating Disorders Association) Conference in Los Angeles and I was delighted to discover a session about exploring the interconnections between sexual orientation and eating disorders, given by Courtney Long (MSW, LC, CHt) of Phoenix, Arizona. Courtney shared that her own personal experience with EDs began in her early teens. She had a lot of the risk factors already such as a controlling mother with rigid rules, black-and-white thinking, perfectionism, and suppression of emotions in the family. Around the same time, she had a brief sexual encounter with a female that left her confused and doubting herself for years, always feeling like there was *something wrong with her* that she couldn't quite put her finger on. She began exercising compulsively, cutting, restricting her food, and her ED behaviors got more and more serious.

Fast forward to adulthood, and one day, Courtney met a woman and fell madly in love. At that point, coming out didn't feel like a choice. She knew she couldn't hide her love. Thankfully, her family was very accepting. By accepting her own sexuality and having the support of her family and friends, Courtney then felt she was able to examine her ED behaviors and seek treatment. "I had somehow convinced myself that salad tasted good without dressing," she joked. "I love ranch dressing, and today I eat it whenever I want." Now, Courtney is a life coach, hypnotherapist, author, speaker, and more, all to spread the gospel of self-care, authenticity, fluidity, and acceptance.

Courtney's success story is uplifting, but it's not always the norm. In an environment that's not always supportive and accept-

Despite the notion that eating disorders are less prevalent among homosexual girls than heterosexual girls, studies show that the rates of affliction are roughly the same.

ing, people in sexual minority groups often face additional pressures and challenges that lead to increased self-doubt, shame, and depression. LGBT adolescents are especially at-risk, as they often struggle with accepting their identity, coming out, and fitting in with peers who can be downright cruel. In Courtney's situation, coming out helped her face and get treatment for her ED, but in other cases, coming out could be so stressful (especially when friends and/or family are not supportive) that it could actually intensify ED symptoms. Does authenticity lead to recovery or is it so painful that it can make existing conditions even worse? Courtney says there's not much research out there on the topic; based on her experience, some LGBT folks see these factors as related, while others don't.

Examining the Relationship Between Eating Disorders and Sexual Orientation

So, what about those prevalent assumptions that gay men suffer from EDs much more than straight guys and lesbian women are more "immune" to EDs than heterosexual women? Researchers would say that both of those assumptions stem from a *sociocultural perspective*. For gay men, sociocultural suggestions state that the values and norms in the gay community place a heightened focus on physical appearance, and that by aiming to attract other men, they are subject to similar pressures and demands as heterosexual women (bodies as sexual objects, and thus, increased body dissatisfaction.) Although the sociocultural perspective is only part of the picture, it turns out that homosexual and bisexual men do in fact have significantly increased prevalence of EDs and ED behaviors including increased dieting, greater fear of gaining weight, lower body satisfaction, and dysfunctional beliefs about the importance of body shape. One recent [2007] study found that 6% of gay or bisexual males met the criteria for an eating disorder, compared to 1% of heterosexual males.

The sociocultural explanation for EDs does not hold up as well when it comes to lesbian and bisexual women. The suggestion is that these women do not share the same standards of feminine beauty espoused by western culture that straight women do, and thus, will be less likely to subscribe to the thin ideal and supporting behaviors. In fact, some studies have found lower levels of body dissatisfaction than heterosexual women; however, other studies have shown conflicting results, either finding no difference between heterosexual and lesbian/bisexual women among

Prevalence of Eating Disorders in Gay and Bisexual Men and Women

Percentage of population sample that was diagnosed with an eating disorder over the course of their lifetime.

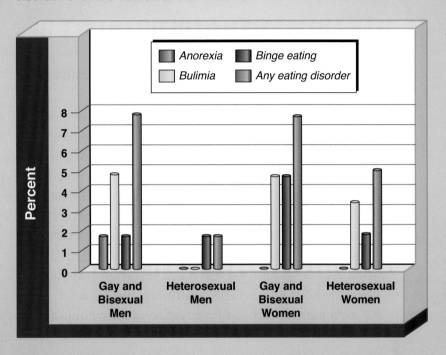

Taken from: Matthew B. Feldman and Ilan H. Meyer, "Eating Disorders in Diverse Lesbian, Gay, and Bisexual Populations," *International Journal of Eating Disorders*, vol. 40, no. 3, April 2007, p. 11.

ED symptoms, or even *higher* levels of EDs (specifically, binge eating disorder) in lesbians compared with straight women. So what gives? This idea that lesbians are immune to EDs just because they supposedly eschew the Barbie beauty standard doesn't seem to fit, especially when you consider that *social* is only one-third of "biopsychosocial," the buzz-phrase in the mental health field for explaining the complex causes behind eating disorders. Sure enough, [Matthew B. Feldman and Ilan H. Meyer's 2007] study (one of the most recent and methodologically sound studies on this subject) found that the prevalence of EDs among lesbians and bisexual women is comparable to heterosexual women. Although the sociocultural factors associated with being a sexual minority can *increase* risk factors for EDs (as with gay and bisexual men), the positive aspects may not be enough to actually *decrease* risk factors substantially (as we see here with bisexual/lesbian women.)

Body Dissatisfaction Among Transgender Individuals

As for transgender individuals, they often feel tremendous body dissatisfaction. As Courtney put it, "There is so much body dissatisfaction in our society today anyway. Just imagine if you also felt like you were born into completely the wrong body." Not surprisingly, there is a dearth of research on EDs among transgender individuals, a population lacking in research overall. One attendee in Courtney's session mentioned that brand new research has found that transgender people with EDs who go through transition recover from their ED based solely on the transition. So, when the body dissatisfaction subsides, the ED tends to go away. An intriguing idea, but I have yet to see the published study so I'm on the lookout for it. To the contrary, another session attendee, who frequently worked with homeless transgender teens and young adults at a center in New York City, stated that she often saw male-to-female transgender people develop EDs as they were transitioning because they felt the need to be delicate, feminine, skinny, and small. Also, being young and uneducated, many of them felt like the only work they could get was sex work, so "passing" was a big deal. They perceived that "passing" as female was the only way to be attractive as a sex worker, the only way to get the money to pay for gender reassignment surgery, so if "passing" meant extreme weight loss, it was a risk they felt they had to take.

At the end of the day, research on eating disorders among people who identify as LGBT is still insufficient and conflicting. However, based on the research we *do* have, it's clear that some segments of the LGBT population face increased risk factors for eating disorders and body dissatisfaction. Thus, it is important for mental health practitioners, medical professionals, parents, and educators not to buy in to the assumptions that lesbian and bisexual women are less vulnerable to eating disorders than straight women, or that just because EDs are more common in gay men that they never affect straight men. Although some *people* unfortunately still discriminate on the basis of sexuality or gender identity, eating disorders do not.

For Boys with Eating Disorders, Finding Treatment Can Be Hard

Rhitu Chatterjee

Although eating disorders are commonly associated with women, an estimated 10 million men in the United States have battled a form of the illness. In the following viewpoint Rhitu Chatterjee reports on the lack of eating disorder treatment tailored for men. She relates the experiences of two adolescent boys who found treatment at the only US residential program for boys and men suffering from eating disorders. Chatterjee is a journalist based in Delhi, India, who has written articles for *Science* magazine and produced radio pieces for National Public Radio.

Last year, Kathy Noyes began to notice that her 12-year-old son, Jonathan, was eating more than usual. She caught him eating late at night. She found empty peanut butter jars and chip and cookie bags stashed around the house.

She didn't know what to make of it. Her friends said, "Well, my boys eat a lot too. They're growing boys. Just wait till you get your grocery bill when they're 16."

But Jonathan soon started to be sent home from school frequently because he was sick.

"He started vomiting a lot," recalls Noyes. "And then afterward he'd be fine. He wasn't feverish, he wasn't pale. So I'd send him back to school and he'd be sick again."

While eating disorders are commonly associated only with females, it is estimated that 10 million American men suffer from them.

That's when she realized something was seriously wrong. She took Jonathan to a doctor who diagnosed him with the eating disorder bulimia nervosa.

Eating disorders are commonly thought to be a problem for girls and women, but an estimated 10 million American men have an eating disorder at some point in their lives, according to the National Eating Disorders Association. Psychologists and psychiatrists who treat eating disorders say those numbers are on the rise. The condition can be life-threatening.

"Over the last five, six years, I've been seeing younger and younger boys who are struggling with these problems," says Roberto Olivardia, a clinical psychologist affiliated with Harvard Medical School, who has been working with boys and men with eating disorders for nearly two decades.

Like girls with eating disorders, the boys tend to be perfectionists and may have mental health problems, including obsessive compulsive disorder, anxiety or depression. Eating disorders tend to kick in during especially difficult life changes.

Jonathan Noyes began binge eating three years ago, when he was 10. He and his family had returned from a vacation when his whole life seemed to fall apart. His father lost his job, which added stress to his parents' relationship. His grandmother got diagnosed with cancer and moved in with his family. And his cat died.

The first food he binged on was peanut butter.

"At first I thought I could stop doing it whenever I want; it's not a big deal," Jonathan says. "You know, it's just a thing I do." But soon he realized "I can't stop this. I'm helpless. I need peanut butter."

That need brought with it an overwhelming sense of guilt, he says. So he started purging. Every time he felt he had overeaten, he says he would lock himself in the bathroom and stick his fingers in his throat until he threw up.

"I felt the relief, but there was still the guilt and pain there," Jonathan says.

He has always been a little chubby and has been bullied at school for it. "I'm the butt of jokes," he says. "I'm the guy that everyone makes fun of."

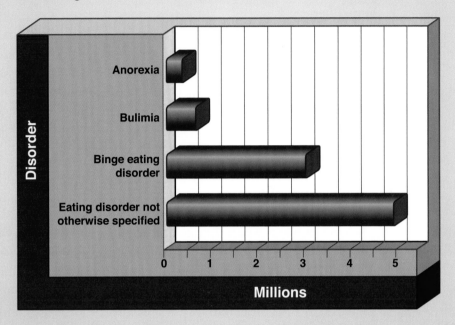

Eating Disorders Among Males

Ten million men in the United States will suffer from a clinically significant eating disorder at some time in their life.

Disorder

- Anorexia
- Bulimia
- Binge eating disorder
- Eating disorder not otherwise specified

Millions

0 1 2 3 4 5

Taken from: "Silent Epidemic?: Eating Disorders Among Males," National Eating Disorders Association, 2012.

Increased social pressure for boys and men to be lean and muscular is at least partly responsible for the rise in males with eating disorders, Olivardia says. "In the early '80s, there was this real significant increase of advertising showing shirtless men, where the body became more of a commodity."

Even comic-book superheroes and GI Joe toys have become more muscular in recent years, Olivardia says.

And though eating disorders in boys share many similarities with those in girls, treatment programs tailored to girls may not feel like the right fit.

Jonathan was the only male patient at an eating disorder program at Hartford Hospital in Connecticut. "A lot of the stuff didn't really apply to me," he says. "Like the stuff about body image, and how you feel, and what's going on in your head and stuff."

"I don't know what it is, but something about having an eating disorder as a boy and having an eating disorder as a girl makes it very different."

Still, the program helped. Jonathan feels better about his own body. He no longer purges, and for the most part doesn't binge.

Collin Schuster lived with eating disorders for six years before finding a treatment program designed for boys and men.

The lack of eating disorders treatment tailored for boys and men is all too familiar to psychiatrist Theodore Weltzin, the director of the nation's only residential program for boys and men, at Rogers Memorial Hospital, a nonprofit psychiatric hospital in Oconomowoc, Wis.

"One of the biggest concerns for men is they feel a little bit like a fish out of water when they go and seek treatment for an eating disorder," says Weltzin.

Collin Schuster entered the program at Rogers Memorial Hospital after six years of bingeing. When he first walked into a room full of boys and men, he felt a weight lift off his shoulders.

"I didn't realize that there were other guys out there who were struggling with similar issues," says Schuster, 18. "That was the start of, OK, maybe this is something that's more common or more manageable than I thought."

Earlier this year, Schuster returned home from the program to Old Saybrook, Conn. When he learned that another boy in his hometown was also struggling with an eating disorder, Schuster reached out to him; he called Jonathan Noyes.

The two now meet regularly. Over video games they talk about their struggles with eating disorders. Schuster has become a friend and a mentor to Noyes, now 13.

Jonathan says that friendship has made him much more confident that he will recover. "It's been difficult, but I'll make it through. I know I will."

ELEVEN

The Anorexic Mindset Is Difficult to Change

Pamela Paul

> In the following viewpoint Pamela Paul explores anorexia recovery. Anorexia is a chronic condition, the author maintains, and only one-third of anorexics are able to recover. The author relates the experience of a woman who has battled anorexia and details the illness' varying levels of recovery. Paul is an award-winning author who has written for the *Atlantic*, the *Washington Post*, the *New York Times*, the *Economist*, *Vogue*, and *Psychology Today*.

Eileen Zyko Wolter was always a chunky child. Growing up as one of four in Connecticut, first in Waterbury and later in Middlebury, she was the good girl, dutifully cleaning off her plate to help compensate for her sister, only eleven months older and a picky eater. In her sister's shadow, Wolter made up for a lack of attention with food. By the time she entered high school, she weighed 201 pounds. "I always turned to food for comfort," she recalls. "I'd come home, unwrap a Hostess snack cake, and sit myself in front of the TV."

When her sister left for college, Wolter had a realization: "I did not want to go to college fat." At seventeen, she went on her first diet. When she graduated from high school, the five-foot-seven

Wolter was 50 pounds lighter. She lost 20 more pounds that summer and, down to 130, she felt ready for freshman year. "I was making the rules," she remembers. "It felt great."

And she wasn't done. While taking classes in film and art history, she subsisted on carrot sticks and peanut butter. Vassar [College] was full of classic type-A girls. "There were lots of women with all kinds of issues there," says Wolter. By the time she came home for Christmas, she weighed only 99 pounds. "I felt like I was really accomplishing something," she says. "It made me feel good to have willpower and say no." Others took notice. "It's that weird trap. Everyone loves it when you lose weight and you look great. But it can be very dangerous."

The next five years were a blur, consumed with intense bouts of anorexia and bulimia, visits to nutritionists, promises to parents and college administrators, lies and relapses. It wasn't until Wolter was 27, with the help of therapy and her boyfriend, who finally said to her, "You're killing yourself," that she felt she had finally freed herself from anorexia.

But what does that really mean? "Personally, I don't think you're ever fully recovered," Wolter, now 41 and living in Summit, New Jersey, says. "It's buried so deep down in there."

Can Anorexia Be Cured?

Wolter, who used to work in the music business and is now a full-time mother of two sons, ages four and seven, will go for days and weeks without succumbing to old patterns. "But then something happens, and it's the first place I go," she admits. "I still look at models and think, Why can't that be me? I don't think it will ever go away. I'll be 90 years old in a nursing home and I'll be like, Is the water aerobics happening?"

Thirty years after the tragic death of Karen Carpenter, we've become familiar with the typical anorexia trajectory. How a young girl, often an overachiever, decides she needs to lose weight. How what may begin as a typical preadolescent fixation on appearance soon turns into habits, a pattern, and finally an obsession.

Patterns of Recovery in Individuals with Anorexia Nervosa and Bulimia Nervosa

Percentage of individuals with eating disorders who met the criteria for recovery at ten and fifteen years from the onset of the disorder

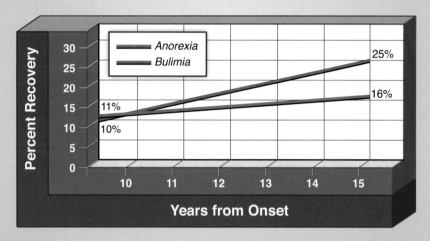

Taken from: Ann Von Holle et al., "Temporal Patterns of Recovery Across Eating Disorder Subtypes," The Royal Australian and New Zealand College of Psychiatrists, 2008. http://eatingdisorders.ucsd.edu.

With the help of therapists and specialists, many girls eventually return to a healthy weight. The consensus in the medical community is that among women with anorexia, roughly 10 percent will die of the disease, one third will remain ill their entire lives, and the remainder will recover to varying degrees. A 1999 longitudinal study out of Harvard that followed 246 anorexic and bulimic women after seven and a half years found that while nearly three-fourths of bulimics were able to resume a normal life, only 33 percent of anorexics were able to do the same. It is often the stresses and weight fluctuations of pregnancy, motherhood, and middle age that cause anorexics to fall back into destructive patterns, raising the question: Once a person has anorexia, is she anorexic forever?

"We still haven't clearly defined what it means to fully recover from anorexia," says Kamryn T. Eddy, Ph.D., assistant professor of psychology at Harvard Medical School and director of the

Harris Center for Education and Advocacy in Eating Disorders. Generally, there are thought to be three components: The first, and most important, is for a woman to regain her weight and her health. Next, she needs to change her patterns of behavior. But the hardest component is the psychological aspect of the disease. It's about a person's thoughts becoming less overwhelmed by thoughts about food, says Eddy. "In a culture in which a certain amount of thinking about weight and shape is pretty normative, what does that actually mean?"

For the anorexic, the world is black-and-white. You are fat or you are thin. You are good or you are bad. You get on the scale and you feel either vindicated or crushed. Eddy talks about recovery in terms of grays. Getting over anorexia, she explains, is about leaving behind a world of clean-cut extremes and navigating life in a much hazier, much harder to manage middle ground.

Falling into Old Habits

Finding that middle ground hasn't been easy for Wolter. After her relationship with the boyfriend who helped her through recovery didn't work out, she eventually went on to marry someone else. Over the years, she has remained in therapy.

She was determined when she first got pregnant to put her eating problems behind her. But gaining weight wasn't easy. "It was horrifying," Wolter recalls. "I had all these friends who loved pregnancy and reveled in their bodies and the growing baby inside them, but I struggled the entire time." She also knew that everyone—family members, her husband, her therapist, her doctors—was watching her. So though she exercised as much as possible, she ate the same way most women do throughout pregnancy—a lot. It was almost like she had to prove to herself and to her minders: I'm fine! Really. But was she? "When I got to the doctor's office and the scale read 205 pounds, I thought, Oh, my God, how am I going to lose this weight?"

Women who have had an eating disorder have widely different experiences with pregnancy. While some say pregnancy helps with their recoveries, teaching them to see that their bodies can bring life rather than destroy their own, others relapse into disordered eating, a rare occurrence referred to as "pregorexia."

Wolter was in that nebulous area—she was able to eat healthfully, but quietly obsessed over her weight gain. After her son was born, in 2005, she lost her pregnancy pounds very rapidly and started to dip below her prepregnancy weight. Worse, she fell into her old anorexic habits. If she ate a handful of her son's Goldfish or Cheerios, she'd spend the day castigating herself. "Fifty calories!" She would clear the snacks out of the house to prevent future transgressions. Rather than take a bus, she would power-push her son's stroller for miles. "It was all the same old unhealthy thought patterns: I can control my food! Size 28 jeans!"

A Chronic Condition

Anorexia has long been considered a chronic condition. Some women, like 34-year-old Becca Sterner, a computer trainer and mother of two from Pennsylvania, calls herself "in recovery" after years of illness and inpatient treatment during college. "I truly believe

For sufferers of anorexia nervosa, the reality of thinness often gets greatly warped in the pursuit of an unrealistic body image.

anorexia is something that will be with me my entire life, even if I can control it," she said. "It's similar to any other addiction."

But while an alcoholic can decide to stop drinking and a compulsive gambler can stay away from the casino, an anorexic still needs to eat every day, several times a day, for the rest of her life. "Can you live life without anorexia after having anorexia? Absolutely," says Lara Pence, Psy.D., director of alumni affairs at the Renfrew Center, a network of residential eating-disorder clinics. "But it's up to each individual to define what it looks like."

Today, Wolter does not have active anorexia—but she doesn't rule out its return. "There are times when I feel like I'm out of control and it's easier not to eat." Not eating helps her shut out difficult feelings. For Wolter and other women who have struggled with anorexia, parenthood is often the motivating factor behind recovery. She desperately wants to teach her sons that all girls and women aren't crazy about their weight.

Some recovering anorexics become nutritionists or eating-disorder therapists. They tend to adopt stringent behaviors around eating, whether it's a raw diet or a gluten-free regimen. Some eating-disorder specialists say dieting is impossible for a former anorexic and that anyone who has had a problem shouldn't even keep a scale in the house.

Wolter does own a scale, but where she once weighed herself three times a day, she tries not to step on it more than once a week. She goes to Pilates several times a week and eats a varied diet and three full meals a day. Everything in moderation, she'll tell her children. "You can't have chocolate every day, and Mommy can't have chocolate every day." Yet there are always sources of worry, and research shows that stressful life events—moves, job changes, deaths, divorce—are the most common causes for relapse, a fact that Wolter, who is in the process of divorcing her husband, is well aware of.

Martina Verba, who has a doctorate in social work and is a psychotherapist in Westchester who treats women with eating disorders, believes in what she calls the full-enough recovery. "Many women recover enough that they can enjoy full and happy lives," she says. "But there is always going to be a tiny speck of disordered thinking."

According to Verba, the path from partial recovery to full-enough recovery is a gradual one. Defining yourself outside of anorexia. Letting go of rigidity. Ultimately, she says, it's about reconnection.

"I do worry about my eating disorder coming back," Wolter admits. "But I need to be strong for the boys, so I won't let it."

TWELVE

Eating Disorder Recovery Involves Changing One's Self-Image

Meg Haston

In the following viewpoint Meg Haston details her experience in a treatment center for eating disorders. Haston entered the center believing that she suffered from anorexia but was surprised to receive a diagnosis for bulimia nervosa. She learned that recovery involved accepting her diagnosis, grieving for the loss of her eating disorder, and changing her self-image. Meg Haston is a therapist and author who focuses her writing on positive body image.

"Tell me a bit about what brings you here." The psychiatrist across the table has an interested, if professionally detached, demeanor. Points for this, as I know he spends his days asking the exact same question of a population of women largely similar to me: White. Privileged. Angry. . . .

I answer as simply as I can: "I'm anorexic." I have accomplished something that no one can take from me: I am Thin. I am Sick. And still, I am not as accomplished as many of the other women around the lodge, these students, professionals, mothers—largely middle or upper-middle class, given the astronomical cost of treatment. (Inpatient treatment can cost upwards of $3,000 per day; we are all here for 45 days minimum.) In and around the lodge, these women spend their hours between individual and group therapy sessions, equine and art therapy, and meals and snacks. I watch them. Crossing the lawn, reading and journaling beneath the sparse palm trees that border the lodge, are women thinner than me.

Viewing the Competition

Frantic, I categorize my competitors. There are the walking-dead women, with feeding tubes snaking from their nostrils and the hunched walk that says they want to disappear. They are Better Than Me. Stronger. There are women with bodies similar to mine:

painfully thin but without feeding tubes or wheelchairs. Our worth is equal. And there are women who take up more space than me, who are not disciplined enough to be anorexic. They are Less Than. I recognize bulimia and half-assed anorexia when I see them: bodies that might seem "normal" to others but are actually fat. (I consider myself an excellent judge of reality, of course.)

"Tell me about your family." While the psychiatrist takes notes, I rattle off my personal history. Eldest, perfectionist child of high-achieving parents. Genetic predisposition to anxiety, depression, and addiction. Tortured romantic relationship with a man I love desperately but will never have. It's the perfect storm. Genetics has loaded the gun; environment has pulled the trigger.

"And can you talk a little bit about your symptoms?"

This is my time to shine. I tell him that I have been restricting myself to around 300 calories a day, but that I don't generally go more than a day without eating. (There are women here who could boast up to three days on water and cigarettes alone. I've never been more envious of anything in my life.) I tell him that I purge all regular meals and most restricted meals. And then, ashamed, I mention the occasional binge episode: periods of time in which I eat everything around me, induce vomiting, go out to buy more food, and repeat the cycle. I don't know how long these episodes last or how much I consume. I know only this: For a fleeting moment after I purge, I feel calm. Relaxed. I can best describe it as a brief, sweet release from my life. It's what everyone here is looking for.

"All right." The psychiatrist takes a few more notes, then releases his pen to the notepad. I lean forward, waiting for The Verdict. The confirmation that I am good enough.

Receiving the Diagnosis

"Considering your history and symptoms, I'm diagnosing you with bulimia nervosa."

No. This is a mistake. "Bulimia?" I choke. It's the bad diagnosis, the label that means I am impulsive, weak. I want my old identity back. In less than five seconds, this man has erased me.

Bulimia nervosa sufferers often experience uncontrollable binge and purge cycles, in which they consume a large amount of food and quickly vomit it back up.

"You don't meet the diagnostic criteria for anorexia nervosa, given that you're still menstruating," he explains. Right. I know this. I make a few quick mental calculations: It will probably take only a few more pounds for me to lose my period. I've been fighting to do that anyway, to rid myself of the one final reminder that I am a woman and that I am alive.

He tells me that it is time to choose. That every moment I am making a choice for Recovery—for health—or for my eating disorder. He tells me that there are no other choices. He is right. I can opt for health, for life. Or I can continue to find my identity in my illness, can work for the diagnosis for which I am literally dying. It's the ultimate choice: life or death.

I am still reeling a week later, and not only from the diagnosis. They have taken everything from me here, and I can feel the anger growing. It gets a little thicker every time a staff member stares at me while I pick at my meal. Every time I have to ask a nurse for a tampon (we are allowed only one tampon at a time, supposedly to prevent us from soaking them in water and swallowing them to fake weight gain). Every time I have to ask a staff member to flush the toilet for me, as we are not permitted to flush on our own.

Accepting Treatment

This afternoon, I am on my way to bulimic group therapy. *I'll humor them*, I tell myself. *But I'm not like these people*. I'm riding in the back of a golf cart since the hospital bracelet on my wrist is stamped with a T, for transport. Given my low weight, I am not permitted to walk to group on my own.

Bulimic group is held in the kitchen of a small house on the grounds, around a long wooden table. For some of us, the kitchen table is the only place we have ever been able to exert control, and the place we most fear losing it. For others, the kitchen is linked with memories of trauma. For all of us, it is a terrifying place to be.

The other women and I know the second we step through the doors that something is horribly wrong. Our chatter stops the instant the sickeningly sweet smell registers in our psyches: a combination of baking cinnamon rolls, frosting, and melted chocolate. My stomach lurches. I wonder whether I could outrun a golf cart.

"Come on in, ladies." Our dietitian and one of the therapists are standing next to the kitchen counter, which is packed with every snack food imaginable. "Today is our binge-food experiential."

Peanut butter, chocolate, cakes, and cookies: The assortment is literally dizzying. I grip the edge of the kitchen table, hard. I can't do this. Next to me, one of the women starts to cry.

Somehow, we all find our way to a seat around the table. Our dietitian explains: We are to take a small amount of our favorite foods typical of a binge. We are meant to taste it, to show ourselves that we are capable of enjoying food, neither avoiding it entirely nor consuming all of it. For many psychologically healthy women, such a task might be enjoyable. The smells might evoke pleasant memories of time with family or friends. Special occasions. But I am instantly transported back to my worst binge/purge episode in recent months. . . .

"Meg?" The dietitian prompts me. "Will you choose some food, please?"

She's kind, and I want to bean her with one of these pies. She's not just asking me to eat. She's asking me to value myself enough to stay alive.

Stomach clenched, I choose a scoop of ice cream and a bit of cookie dough. *I'll choose Recovery tomorrow. Just don't make me do this.* I'm a glutton for punishment, I suppose: This is the same food I chose during my binge episode. But my experience of it now could not be more different. I am sitting at a table instead of standing in my kitchen in the dark. I am with others who understand exactly why this is so frightening. And after a week or so of regular meals, I'm thinking more clearly. I'm thinking that maybe I am capable of change. . . .

I lift my spoon and take a bite.

Recovery Is a Grieving Process

"IT'S A GRIEVING PROCESS." My body-image therapist, a beautiful woman with an enviable comfort in her own curvy flesh, is sitting next to me. "When you make the choice for Recovery, you have to grieve the loss of your eating disorder, like losing a close friend."

The shame I feel for my tears makes it impossible to look at her. "I want my old body back." Already there is softness where there was none before, a sway to my hips that betrays my womanness. "This body isn't mine."

"It is," she corrects me gently. "It just takes time to accept it, to relearn it."

I know she's right. We have just finished an exercise in which I have shaped pieces of string into what I believe to be the circumference of my thighs, hips, and waist. I learned that I view myself to be at least 50 pounds heavier than I actually am. How can I begin to accept a new body, a new relationship with myself, when my view of myself is so horribly distorted?

So this is the real work that begins in the hours, days, months, and years after treatment. To grieve the loss of my illness just as I do the loss of my relationship, of what I thought both could do for me. To allow myself to feel anger, sadness, and betrayal. To accept that health means softness and curves, embracing my identity as a woman.

The grieving process is not linear; there are still many days when I long for my old body or am tempted to cope with life's stresses in unhealthy ways. But I am learning. I am learning to celebrate my identity as a writer, a daughter, and a sister, instead of a sick woman. To nurture with gratitude a body that can move and make love and, should I choose, bear a child. I am a Recovering Woman who makes a choice for health every day. Because there is no other choice.

What You Should Know About Eating Disorders

Facts About Eating Disorders

- 20 million women and 10 million men in the United States suffer from an eating disorder at some time in their lives.
- 95 percent of eating disorder sufferers are between ages twelve and twenty-five.
- Almost half of all Americans know someone who has suffered from an eating disorder.
- Eating disorders are most common in English-speaking countries and in Europe, but rates are increasing in non-Western countries.
- 85 to 90 percent of eating disorder sufferers are female.
- Eating disorders have the highest mortality rate of any mental illness.
- The eating disorder risk is higher for athletes, especially in sports emphasizing appearance, weight requirements, and muscularity.
- Children as young as five have been diagnosed with eating disorders.

Anorexia

- The third most common chronic illness among adolescents is anorexia.
- 1 to 4 percent of women suffer from anorexia in their lifetime.

- In a 2011 study, almost 2 percent of teens ages thirteen to eighteen had anorexia or near-anorexia.
- 33 percent of people with anorexia recover fully, 33 percent go between recovery and relapse periods, and 33 percent remain very ill or die. Suicide and cardiac arrest are the most common causes of death.
- The mortality rate of anorexia nervosa is twelve times higher than the death rate associated with all other causes of death for females ages fifteen to twenty-four years old.

Bulimia

- 1.1 to 4.2 percent of women have bulimia nervosa in their lifetime.
- In a 2011 study, about 1 percent of teens ages thirteen to eighteen had bulimia.
- 41 percent of bulimic teens reported purging, while the others used other behaviors to compensate for eating.
- About 75 percent of women with bulimia will recover fully and almost all will recover to some extent.
- About 50 percent of people who have had anorexia develop bulimia or bulimic patterns.
- Almost 4 percent of bulimia sufferers will die of health complications stemming from the disease.

Binge Eating Disorder

- An estimated 3.5 percent of females and 2 percent of men in the United States suffer from binge eating disorder.
- In a 2011 study, 4 percent of teens ages thirteen to eighteen suffered from binge eating disorder or binge eating that did not meet criteria in the *Diagnostic and Statistical Manual of Mental Disorders, Fifth Edition*.
- 43 percent of individuals with binge eating disorder will receive treatment.
- 5.2 percent of individuals suffering from EDNOS (eating disorders not otherwise specified) die from complications related to the disorder.

Treatment for Eating Disorders

- About 60 percent of people with eating disorders recover fully, 20 percent recover partially, and 20 percent do not recover and die early from their illness.
- The most effective treatment for eating disorders includes psychological counseling, attention to a sufferer's nutritional needs, and sometimes medications such as antidepressants.
- Cognitive behavioral therapy, in which patients learn to identify and change unhelpful thought patterns, is a recommended therapy for bulimia and binge eating disorder.
- 43.6 percent of those with binge eating disorder receive treatment, 33.8 percent of those with anorexia receive treatment, and 43.2 percent of those with bulimia receive treatment.
- Programs specializing in eating disorders treat only 35 percent of eating disorder sufferers.
- It costs an average of $30,000 a month to attend a residential treatment program. Patients often stay for three or more months.
- Outpatient treatment can total $100,000 or more.
- Most insurers do not cover long-term eating disorder treatment.
- From 1999 to 2009 hospitalizations for eating disorders grew for all age groups. Rates for children under twelve increased 72 percent, and rates for adults ages forty-five to sixty-five grew by 88 percent. Eighty-eight percent of those hospitalized between 2008 and 2009 were women.

What You Should Do About Eating Disorders

Learn the Facts

Learn what you are talking about before you form an opinion, write a paper, take a stand, or talk with a friend about eating disorders. There is a lot of information out there about eating disorders, and, thanks to the Internet, much of this information is at your fingertips. But bear in mind that anybody can put up a website, start an organization, or write a blog, whether they are informed about the topic or not. Therefore, it is very important to evaluate whether or not what you read is believable. To do this, seek out sources such as government sites, major organizations, well-known newspapers, news sites, and periodicals. Even then, double check the information you find with several other sources. Look at when information is posted, choosing the most recent. Checking dates is especially important when dealing with scientific information, such as statistics and research about eating disorders. Evaluate the tone of the source. Is it well written? Does it seem objective, or does it show a clear bias? Blogs often provide great perspectives and opinions that you might not find elsewhere, but be cautious about relying on them for factual information.

Take Action

If you think you may have an eating disorder, the first step to recovery is admitting that something is wrong. Then, it is vital to talk to someone about your concerns. This may be very difficult, but it is an important step in getting the help you may need. Choose someone trustworthy and nonjudgmental—it could be a close friend, family member, minister, rabbi, imam, sports coach, youth group leader, or teacher. The next step is seeing a health care professional, who will run tests, make a diagnosis, and help you find treatment.

If you're concerned about a friend's eating behaviors or attitudes, find a private place where you can talk with the friend and not be interrupted. Be specific about your concerns—say exactly what you have observed and tell your friend you are worried. It is *not* helpful to make comments about body shape and weight, such as, "You're so thin." Do not judge your friend. Do not be a know-it-all ("If you'd just stop eating so much, you'd be OK"). Ask open-ended questions such as, "What would make you feel better?" and "Is there anything I can do to help you right now?" Let your friend talk, listening carefully. Let your friend know you are there for him or her. Offer to be present while he or she calls the help lines, such as those run by the National Eating Disorders Association (NEDA) or the National Association of Anorexia Nervosa and Associated Disorders (ANAD). Set up an appointment with a therapist or doctor or accompany your friend to an appointment. If your friend says nothing is wrong or gets angry, you may need to talk with an adult you trust. This may feel like you are betraying your friend, but part of being there for someone you love is taking action to help him or her heal.

Raise Your Voice

If eating disorders are an important issue for you, there are ways you can inform and help others. Organizations such as NEDA and ANAD have sections on their websites about how to help. For example, NEDA sponsors walks all over the country to raise awareness, bring together communities, and fund-raise. You can become a media watchdog, notifying the organization when you see messages that promote unhealthy food behaviors. You can host speakers or movie nights at schools, libraries, or community events. You can even host a scale-smashing or build a life-size Barbie display! If you have recovered from an eating disorder, you can become a great resource for others. Through NEDA and ANAD, you can talk with and support people who are battling eating disorders, become a speaker, or lobby legislators for better laws protecting eating disorder sufferers and for more funding to study these diseases.

ORGANIZATIONS TO CONTACT

The editors have compiled the following list of organizations concerned with the issues debated in this book. The descriptions are derived from materials provided by the organizations. All have publications or information available for interested readers. The list was compiled on the date of publication of the present volume; the information provided here may change. Be aware that many organizations take several weeks or longer to respond to inquiries, so allow as much time as possible.

About-Face
PO Box 191145
San Francisco, CA 94119
(415) 839-6779
website: www.about-face.org

Founded in 1995, About-Face is a nonprofit organization that aims to equip women and girls with tools to resist harmful media messages that affect their self-esteem and body image. About-Face hosts media-literacy workshops and body-image programs in schools, organizations, and communities in the San Francisco Bay area. The organization's website offers pages on topics such as body image, media, eating disorders and disordered eating, self-esteem and mental health, and health and weight.

Academy for Eating Disorders (AED)
111 Deer Lake Road, Suite 100
Deerfield, IL 60015
(847) 498-4274 • fax: (847) 480-9282
email: info@aedweb.org
website: www.aedweb.org

AED is a global association committed to leadership in eating disorder research, education, treatment, and prevention. The mission of AED is to generate knowledge about eating disorders, provide platforms for the promotion of eating disorder research, and build capacity for the next generation of eating disorders professionals. The association publishes the *International Journal of Eating Disorders* and the *AED Forum Newsletter*.

Alliance for Eating Disorders Awareness
1649 Forum Place #2
West Palm Beach, FL 33401
(561) 841-0900
email: info@allianceforeatingdisorders.com
website: www.allianceforeatingdisorders.com

Founded in 2000, the Alliance for Eating Disorders Awareness is a nonprofit organization dedicated to providing programs related to eating disorders, positive body image, and self-esteem. The organization provides educational presentations, support groups, advocacy for mental health legislation, and a toll-free national phone help line. The alliance also offers referrals, training, support, and mentoring services. The aim of the organization is to share the message that it is possible to recover from eating disorders, and that individuals should not have to suffer or recover alone.

Binge Eating Disorder Association (BEDA)
637 Emerson Place
Severna Park, MD 21146
(855) 855-2332 • fax: (410) 741-3037
website: www.bedaonline.com

BEDA is a national organization that focuses on providing leadership, recognition, prevention, and treatment of BED (binge eating disorder). The organization facilitates increased awareness and proper diagnosis of BED through outreach, education, and advocacy. BEDA hosts an annual conference, which features workshops and networking opportunities with clinicians, researchers, individuals with BED and their families, advocates, and educators.

Eating Disorders Anonymous (EDA)
PO Box 55876
Phoenix, AZ 85078-5876
email: info@eatingdisordersanonymous.org
website: www.eatingdisordersanonymous.org

EDA is an organization that helps individuals recover from their eating disorders. It provides a fellowship of individuals who share their experiences in order to solve their common problems. There are no dues or fees for EDA membership; the organization survives through self-supporting contributions. EDA is not allied with any sect, denomination, political party, organization, or institution. The organization does not promote diets or weight management techniques. EDA endorses sound nutrition and discourages any form of rigidity around food. The organization has chapters around the world; if members are not able to attend an in-person meeting, EDA offers online chat and phone meetings as well.

Eating Disorders Coalition (EDC)
720 7th Street NW, Suite 300
Washington, DC 20001
(202) 543-9570
email: manager@eatingdisorderscoalition.org
website: www.eatingdisorderscoalition.org

EDC is an advocacy organization for eating disorders. Its goal is to advance the recognition of eating disorders as a public health priority in the United States. The organization aims to raise awareness among policy makers and the public about eating disorders, promote federal support for improved access to eating disorder treatment, and increase funding for scientific research on eating disorders. EDC mobilizes citizens to advocate on behalf of people with eating disorders, their families, and professionals in the field.

Families Empowered and Supporting Treatment of Eating Disorders (F.E.A.S.T.)
PO Box 11608
Milwaukee, WI 53211

(855) 50-FEAST
email: info@feast-ed.org
website: http://members.feast-ed.org

F.E.A.S.T. is an international organization for parents and care-givers of individuals with eating disorders. The organization provides support and information for people to help their loved ones recover from eating disorders. F.E.A.S.T. promotes evidence-based treatment and advocates for research and education to reduce the suffering associated with eating disorders. F.E.A.S.T. has members in forty-one countries.

FINDINGbalance
PO Box 284
Franklin, TN 37065
(615) 599-6948
website: www.findingbalance.com

FINDINGbalance is a Christian resource for individuals dealing with eating and body image issues. The mission of the organization is to provide resources to help people live healthier, more balanced lives. FINDINGbalance develops programs and services rooted in biblical principles to help individuals with eating disorders. The organization's website offers an online support program, blog, and information on disordered eating. FINDINGbalance hosts the annual Hungry for Hope conference, which features workshops on disordered eating, clinical teaching, and worship.

National Association of Anorexia Nervosa and Associated Disorders (ANAD)
750 E. Diehl Road #127
Naperville, IL 60563
(630) 577-1333 • help line: (630) 577-1330
email: anadhelp@anad.org
website: www.anad.org

ANAD is a nonprofit corporation that seeks to prevent and ease problems associated with eating disorders. It promotes eating disorder awareness, prevention, and recovery by supporting and educating individuals, families, and professionals. The organization offers an eating disorder help line and its website provides links to treatment centers, support groups, online forums, news updates, and information about legislative advocacy.

National Eating Disorders Association (NEDA)
165 West 46th Street, Suite 402
New York, NY 10036
(212) 575-6200
email: info@nationaleatingdisorders.org
website: www.nationaleatingdisorders.org

NEDA is a US nonprofit that advocates on behalf of individuals and families affected by eating disorders. The organization campaigns for prevention, improved access to treatment, and increased research funding for eating disorders. The organization offers an eating disorder help line, and the organization's website provides research, webinars, videos, and support groups. NEDA also hosts Proud2BMe, an online community for teens that aims to promote positive body image and encourage healthy attitudes about food and weight.

National Institute of Mental Health (NIMH)
6001 Executive Blvd., Room 6200, MSC 9663
Bethesda, MD 20892-9663
(301) 443-4513 • toll-free: (866) 615-6464 • fax: (301) 443-4279
email: nimhinfo@nih.gov
website: www.nimh.nih.gov

NIMH works to transform the understanding and treatment of mental illnesses. The mission of NIMH is to pave the way for the prevention, recovery, and cure of mental illnesses through research. It supports research studies on eating disorders, and its findings are available on the institute's website. The website also features a section on eating disorders that provides research and science news.

BIBLIOGRAPHY

Books

Laurie Halse Anderson, *Wintergirls*. New York: Viking, 2009.

Stephanie Covington Armstrong, *Not All Black Girls Know How to Eat: A Story of Bulimia*. Chicago: Lawrence Hill, 2009.

Carrie Arnold, *Decoding Anorexia: How Breakthroughs in Science Offer Hope for Eating Disorders*. New York: Routledge, 2012.

Lee Wolfe Blum, *Table in the Darkness: A Healing Journey Through an Eating Disorder*. Downers Grove, IL: InterVarsity, 2013.

Harriet Brown, *Brave Girl Eating: A Family's Struggle with Anorexia*. New York: HarperCollins, 2010.

Carolyn Costin and Gwen Schubert Grabb, *8 Keys to Recovery from an Eating Disorder: Effective Strategies from Therapeutic Practice and Personal Experience*. New York: Norton, 2012.

Brian Cuban, *Shattered Image: My Triumph over Body Dysmorphic Disorder*. NetMinds, 2013.

Portia de Rossi, *Unbearable Lightness: A Story of Loss and Gain*. New York: Atria, 2010.

Sunny Sea Gold, *Food: The Good Girl's Drug: How to Stop Using Food to Control Your Feelings*. New York: Penguin, 2011.

Lindsey Hall, *Bulimia: A Guide to Recovery*. Carlsbad, CA: Gurze, 2010.

Nicole Johns, *Purge: Rehab Diaries*. Berkeley, CA: Seal, 2009.

Lois Metzger, *A Trick of the Light*. New York: Balzer + Bray, 2013.

Julie O'Toole, *Give Food a Chance*. Portland, OR: Perfectly Scientific, 2010.

Joanna Poppink, *Healing Your Hungry Heart: Recovering from Your Eating Disorder*. San Francisco: Conari, 2011.

Justine Jeanette Reel, *Eating Disorders: An Encyclopedia of Causes, Treatment, and Prevention*. Santa Barbara, CA: ABC-CLIO, 2013.

Jenni Schaefer, *Goodbye Ed, Hello Me: Recover from Your Eating Disorder and Fall in Love with Life*. New York: McGraw Hill, 2009.

Jennifer Thomas and Jenni Schaefer, *Almost Anorexic: Is My (or My Loved One's) Relationship to Food a Problem?* Center City, MN: Hazelden, 2013.

Ron A. Thompson and Roberta Trattner Sherman, *Eating Disorders in Sport*. New York: Routledge, 2010.

Periodicals and Internet Sources

Rachel Adams, "The Flip Side of Food Studies," *Chronicle of Higher Education*, August 2, 2013.

Laura Beil, "The Snack-Food Trap," *Newsweek*, November 5, 2012.

Cindy Berner, "Disordered Eating in Athletes," *American Fitness*, September–October 2012.

Adi Bloom, "Websites That Feed Anorexia Self-Harm," *Times Educational Supplement*, January 18, 2013.

Sharon Cotliar, "Demi Lovato: 'I'm Fighting Every Day to Be Healthy,'" *People*, May 2, 2011.

Alice Gregory, "Hunger Games," *New Republic*, December 30, 2013.

Kelley King Heyworth, "Kids Who Won't Eat," *Parents*, January 2011.

Marina Khidekel, "Can You Catch an Eating Disorder?," *Seventeen*, March 2010.

Michelle Konstantinovsky, "Not Your Daughter's Eating Disorder," *O, The Oprah Magazine*, May 2013.

Sophia Banay Moura, "Starvation Nation," *Marie Claire*, July 2011.

Jane Shin Park, "Thin Ice: The Internet and Eating Disorders," *Teen Vogue*, September 2009.

Olivia Patrick, "The Problem with Thinstagram," *Dolly*, October 2013.

Nathaniel Penn, "20% of Anorexics Are Men," GQ, September 2012.

Stacey Schultz, "Righteous Eating," *Seattle*, December 2013.

Philip T.B. Starks and Brittany L. Slabach, "The Scoop on Eating Dirt," *Scientific American*, June 2012.

Kim Tranell, "The Secret New Eating Disorder," *Seventeen*, April 2011.

Emily Troscianko, "Portrait of a Hunger Artist," *Psychology Today*, March–April 2010.

Bonnie Vaughan, "The Rise of the Healthy Eating Disorder," *Good Health*, December 2013.

INDEX

PICTURE CREDITS